Clellan Card, the star of *Axel and His Dog*

Clellan Card is remembered by millions of Minnesotans as Axel Torgeson, the nutty Scandihoovian who lived in a tree house. But in addition to his indelible portrayal of Axel, Clellan was a Twin Cities broadcasting pioneer.

- In September 1930, he appeared in the first demonstration of television in the Twin Cities
- In April 1938, he hosted the first radio program broadcast live from the new WCCO radio building
- On April Fools' Day in 1939, a crowd of 1,800 people came to watch Clellan do his radio show – at 7:00 a.m.
- He was the most popular radio personality in the entire upper Midwest in the late 1930s
- At one time or another, he worked at four of the leading radio stations in the Twin Cities: WCCO, KSTP, WDGY, and WTCN
- In October 1954, he appeared in the first local color television broadcast in the Twin Cities, a special episode of *Axel and His Dog*
- In the 1950s, more than 12,000 people attended "Axel Day" each year at Excelsior Amusement Park
- The ratings for *Axel and His Dog* were often more than the other three competing programs combined
- He was named "Best Children's Show Personality" by the Twin Cities chapter of the American Federation of Television and Radio Artists (AFTRA) numerous times
- In 2002, Clellan Card was posthumously inducted into the Pavek Museum of Broadcasting's Hall of Fame

Clellan Card, circa 1941

WHAT A CARD!

The Story of
Clellan Card
and
Axel and His Dog

By
Julian West

Beaver's Pond Press, Inc.

Portions of the text appeared in somewhat different form as "Twin Cities Farewells" in *TV Party! Television's Untold Tales* by Billy Ingram (Chicago & Los Angeles: Bonus Books, 2002).

Most photos are courtesy of the Pavek Museum of Broadcasting and WCCO-TV.

Other photos are courtesy of Michael Card, Don Stolz, WCCO radio, KSTP radio, Syngenta (formerly Northrup, King & Co.), and the Blake School. Illustrations are courtesy of Marc Johnson.

Axel and His Dog programs on the accompanying DVD are courtesy of the Pavek Museum of Broadcasting, WCCO-TV, and Michael Card. "The Night Before Christmas" recording on the DVD is courtesy of WCCO-TV and Allan Lotsberg.

Used by permission.

ISBN 13: 978-1-59298-261-5
ISBN 10: 1-59298-261-1
Library of Congress Control Number: 2008940166
Book design and typesetting: Mighty Media, Inc.
Printed in the United States of America
First Printing: 2009

12 11 10 09 08   5 4 3 2 1

Beaver's Pond Press, Inc.

7104 Ohms Lane, Suite 101
Edina, Minnesota 55439 USA
(952) 829-8818
www.BeaversPondPress.com

To order, visit www.BookHouseFulfillment.com or call 1-800-901-3480. Reseller and special sales discounts available.

For my mom, who always believed in me

Birdie with a yellow bill
Hopped upon my windowsill,
Cocked his shining eye and said:
What's that on your shirt, Axel – grease?
Bee boop!

TABLE OF CONTENTS

Axel illustration by Marc Johnson

FOREWORD

BY LOUIE ANDERSON

ON MANY A FROSTY MINNESOTA MORNING, while my dad was still sleeping or gone to work and my mom was humming a tune and stirring the oatmeal, I'd turn on the TV that we got from the dump, with vise grips for a knob and tin foil on the aerial. Clicking over to "Canal 4," I would follow the camera up the steps of a tree to find a goofy guy wearing a funny-looking hat and an old broom mustache, and I'd happily anticipate his usual cheerful greeting in that funny voice of his. Even though it might have been freezing cold and blowing snow, it always looked like Axel and his friends were spared the bad weather. Boy, that tree house must have been high up!

Axel's zany ways and warm heart could usually take the edge off a twenty-below windchill, anyway. It was really nice to know that no matter how rotten the day before was, I always had a special friend who was never in a bad mood, who had no expectations, and who was full of fun and full of unconditional love.

Axel could make old jokes new and get the biggest laugh out of the smallest gesture. He could make a fake mustache come to life. He was Minnesota's own version of Mr. Rogers – a ridiculous Mr. Rogers, maybe, but he really did have that kind of impact on my generation when we were growing up.

As a kid, I wasn't always sure when Axel was kidding. While my mom was dishing out the oatmeal, she would often chuckle at something he said even though I didn't hear anything that I thought was funny. I think I've gotten a little more sophisticated since then!

I would eagerly repeat Axel's jokes and Birdies to my friends, like "What did you do with your car in St. Louis – park?" And who knows? Maybe way back then, while sitting too close to the TV for my own good, Axel planted a seed in my life that grew into a tree house of a comedy career. To this day, onstage all over the country, I often blurt out that I'm from Minnesnowta, and that always reminds me of Axel.

Axel, a.k.a. Clellan Card, is alive and well in my heart. So when Julian West asked me to write the foreword for this book, I felt that it was Axel reaching down from that big tree house where he must be now, giving me a chance to thank him for warming up my cold, sometimes unhappy, childhood.

This is Louie from Minnesnowta, signing off.

Axel Torgeson

Axel's Tree House illustration re-created by Bill Dietrichson and Steve Jones

"Hɪ, KꞮɒꞩꞮ DꞮꞩꞩ Ɪꞩꞩ ꞱXЕꞱ!"

"Away out in the forest, high in a big tree house, lives our old friend Axel. Let's climb up in the tree house and see what's happening today."

Mᴜᴄʜ ʟɪᴋᴇ "Oɴᴄᴇ ᴜᴘᴏɴ ᴀ ᴛɪᴍᴇ" begins every bedtime fairy tale, those words – recited by a familiar voice emanating from a flickering black-and-white television set – begin a daily ritual throughout the Twin Cities. Happy theme music accompanies the opening narration, while an illustration of a weatherbeaten wooden sign reading "Axel's Tree House" fills the screen. The camera pans to the right, the direction the sign is pointing, to the mammoth trunk of a tree. Then it slowly ascends, following a meandering succession of large, flat steps sticking straight out from the trunk. At the top, a rustic shack, apparently assembled from scraps of lumber, nestles snugly among the branches. A shadowy figure is silhouetted in the large open window. The camera begins to move in, and the picture dissolves to the ramshackle interior of the tree house.

A low, sloping ceiling, patched here and there with irregular boards, gives the place a dilapidated but somehow cozy appearance. In a far corner squats a pot-bellied stove, a teakettle resting on its surface. Off to one side, next to an old rocking chair, stands a swivel blackboard with a message about new chocolate-flavored Malt-o-Meal scrawled across it. Hanging outside a window, a wooden bucket awaits service as a backwoods dumbwaiter. The framed oval portrait of a mutton-chopped ancestor gazes from one wall and on another, in a crude, off-kilter frame, the hoary and sentimental cliché "Home Sweet Home" confers a gently ironic benediction on the scene.

A bizarre cuckoo clock, with the hand-carved head of some fanciful deer-creature staring down from its peak, dominates another wall. Bursting out of the tiny trapdoor above the clock face, a cheerful cuckoo is eternally poised to chirp. Below the clock, large picture windows offer a panoramic view of the outside, where the leaves of the tree ripple and billow in bulbous, cloud-like clumps. Looming in the foreground and placidly dominating the room stands the trunk

Tallulah, Axel, and Towser in September 1959

  What's for breakfast, Ham – hocks?

of the tree, the sawed-off stump of a branch protruding from its side. The wooden box of an old-fashioned wall telephone, its mouthpiece poking out like some alien creature's proboscis, is visible behind the trunk.

Peering around the crotch of the tree is a peculiar-looking fellow. A railroad engineer's cap perches on top of his head, the brim pointing straight up into the air, and bangs hang down over his forehead. A mustache that looks more like bushy nostril hair bristles from beneath his nose. His boldly striped black-and-white T-shirt, intersected at right angles by suspenders, adds to his cartoonish appearance. In addition to suspenders, his pants are also held up by a long rope belt. With his vaguely Hitlerian mustache, the old coot might seem a little forbidding except for the mischievous twinkle in his eyes. Looking directly at the camera, he gives a little wave and exclaims, "Hi, kids! Diss iss Axel!"

From 1954 to 1966, that was the way the most popular local children's television program in Minnesota usually opened. Broadcast in black and white, using a nearly motionless camera, the show featured a goofy host who spoke with a loopy pseudo-Scandinavian accent and told timeworn gags between showings of ancient cartoons and creaky movie shorts. This amalgam of old films, old jokes, and an old geezer was called *Axel and His Dog*.

In the twenty-first century, it might seem hard to believe that such a show could even get on the air – but not only was *Axel and His Dog* broadcast for years, it was a huge hit. Kids of all ages watched regularly, and a lot of adults did, too. At its peak, the program was on five, six, even seven days a week. Axel regularly trounced his competition, often drawing more than twice as many viewers as the runner-up. In May 1957, for example, his audience was 37 percent greater than all three competing programs *combined*.

What were the secrets of Axel's success? Besides a generous helping of jokes and riddles, a typical episode might include insults, arguments, physical violence, drinking, mood-altering drugs – wait a minute! *This* was a children's show?

Well, yes! But the insults and arguments were delivered with tongue firmly in cheek, and the violence was usually nothing more than a playful bop on the noggin, a bucket of water over the head, or a pie in the face. The drinks were "shots of milk" or "Bosco highballs," and the drug of choice was definitely catnip.

There's no mystery about why Axel was popular: he was fun! Axel was a Scandinavian maven of mirth, a goofy guru of gags, and the king of kidvid in Minnesota. Clellan Card, a well-known veteran of Minnesota broadcasting, starred as Axel. He had developed the character years earlier on radio, where he had perfected his dyed-in-the-lutefisk Swedish accent. In the late 1930s, propelled by a large fund of old jokes, Clellan achieved tremendous popularity throughout the upper Midwest with his early morning antics. He was one of the original drive-time DJs, although many of his listeners were walking out to the barn instead of motoring to work. Surveys of radio listeners at the time showed that he was a two-to-one favorite over his competition.

When Axel made the transition from funny radio voice to children's television host, he was so perfect in his new role it seemed surprising that no one had thought of it sooner. On *Axel and His Dog* on WCCO-TV – "Canal Four" as he called it – Axel Torgeson was a goofy hermit who inhabited a tumble-down tree house in the middle of a forest on mythical Magic Island. He absurdly mangled the English language while gleefully telling some of the silliest jokes in history. But he did it with such zest that he was difficult to resist.

Despite the ridiculous nature of the character, Axel seemed somehow real. In contrast with most characters on children's television, he didn't talk down to his audience – he talked *to* them. Effortlessly projecting his personality and warmth through the TV screen, he had a terrific rapport with his viewers. Years later, many fans still recall feeling that Axel, unlike anyone else on television, really seemed to be their friend.

The cheerfully obvious fakery of Axel's Tree House, with a spyglass fashioned out of cardboard tubes, a two-dimensional tree trunk, and a view that was obviously a painted backdrop, didn't trouble young TV watchers, either. Axel lived in the realm of make-believe, something that every child understands. And for adult viewers, *Axel and His Dog* was video vaudeville, a minimalist theater of the absurd. Besides the cornucopia of old chestnuts, the show often contained a liberal dose of in-jokes, double-entendres, and wordplay that few children could have understood.

Much of Axel's repartee was with his dog, Towser, and his cat, Tallulah. Neither "aminal" was ever seen on-screen except for the large

What are you going to do with that turkey – neck?

mottled brown paw of Towser and the dingy white paw of Tallulah. Don Stolz, the locally renowned producer and director of the Old Log Theater, played Axel's strange pets and he made them memorable characters despite their limited visibility. Tallulah spoke in a high, mewling voice, indelibly evoking a high-strung, obnoxious feline. Towser, a gruff but congenial companion, couldn't talk at all – but he barked quite eloquently.

In the later years of the show, Axel was joined by co-host Carmen the Nurse. Played by singer Mary Davies, Carmen brought a dose of sanity to the proceedings – although some speculated about what might be going on after hours between the Scandihoovian recluse and the honey-voiced nurse in the starched white uniform.

Clellan Card as Axel and Mary Davies as Carmen in 1963

Axel and His Dog was produced and directed by Harry Jones, a seasoned WCCO-TV staffer. During much of its twelve-year run, the show was televised live, and Harry had his hands full keeping the unscripted program from disintegrating into chaos. Often, Axel would say whatever popped into his head. Most of the time, his off-the-cuff remarks just triggered spasms of laughter but occasionally they caused headaches behind the scenes.

During Axel's heyday, most of his young fans didn't realize that his alter ego, Clellan Card, had been a mainstay of Minnesota radio and television for more than thirty years. He had been everything from an early morning jester to a late night disc jockey, a zany quizmaster to a suave master of ceremonies. He was responsible for some of the corniest jokes and most excruciating puns that ever tainted the airwaves. Somehow, he made a lot of people laugh, too.

Clellan Card, about age 10

CHAPTER 1

ClelLy

AXEL, CLELLAN CARD'S BEST-KNOWN CHARACTER, was ostensibly Swedish, but Scandinavians were noticeably lacking in Clellan's own ancestry. Isaac Russell Card, his paternal grandfather, was born in Pennsylvania in 1853 to an English–Irish family. Mary Ann Quigley, Clellan's paternal grandmother, was born to Irish parents in Winnipeg, Canada, in 1856. Isaac and Mary were married in 1876 in Hammond, a tiny town in western Wisconsin. Clellan's father, William Harrison Card (or "Daddy Bill," as he was later known to his grandchildren), was born there on November 24, 1878.

In 1892 the Card family, by then including William's brother Delbert and sister Evelyn, moved to Minneapolis, Minnesota, where Isaac Card found work as a beltmaker. Within a few years, he went into business for himself, opening a grocery store at 24th and Bloomington. His family lived there as well, and William, by then a teenager, probably helped out around the store. The young Card also proved to be something of an academic prodigy. In 1895, he graduated from South High School at the age of sixteen. He then entered the College of Dentistry at the University of Minnesota and finished a mere three years later, in the spring of 1898. He was said to be the youngest graduate in the history of the school up to that time.[1] The new dentist soon opened an office in downtown Minneapolis.

William loved music, and in 1900 became a charter member of the Apollo Club, a men's civic group, where he sang bass in the club's choir for a full half-century. His other great passion was golf. Despite the exercise it afforded, however, within a few years the rather stout William had broadened into a comfortably portly figure. By the time he reached middle age, he also sported a well-trimmed mustache.

Clellan's father, William H. Card,
about 1900

Clellan's mother, Ina Covey Card,
about 1900

Ina Covey, the woman who would become William's wife, was born on May 31, 1879, in Bay City, Michigan, on Lake Huron's Saginaw Bay. Her mother (Clellan's maternal grandmother), Mary Alice Rouse, had been born in Athens, New York, in 1847. The Rouse family, like many in New York, was Dutch. Ina's father, Ira J. Covey, born in 1844 in Willet, New York, was descended from English stock. A solicitor and advertising man by trade, he fought on the Union side in the Civil War. (Axel once declared that his grandfather "fought with his Union suit on.") Ira and Mary were wed in 1874. When Ina was about three years old, the family moved to Minneapolis.

Ina and William probably met some time around the turn of the century. They were married on May 29, 1901, two days before Ina's twenty-second birthday. After a honeymoon out East, the newlyweds roomed with William's parents for about a year. By their second anniversary, the Cards were doing well enough to spend $4,990.39 building a home at 2401 Garfield Avenue South in Minneapolis. As a matter of fact, Dr. Card's dental practice was so successful by then that he could even afford thirteen dollars a month for a servant.

On June 24, 1903, shortly before they moved into their new residence, the Cards were dealt a joker: Clellan Covey Card, their only child, was born. This new addition to the family was named after Clellan L. Card, a Philadelphia dentist who perhaps met William at a dentists' function of some sort. The two Cards discovered that they were related and this fact, combined with their shared choice of career, cemented their friendship. "My grandfather and the original Clellan were chums at one point," recalled Clellan's son Michael, "and my grandparents took a liking to the name and laid it on my dad." Clellan L. Card later returned the compliment, naming one of his sons William. (And in turn, the younger William's son, Clellan L. Card, carries the distinctive first name today.) Gaelic or Scottish in origin, Clellan means "clay land," and refers to an area of southern Scotland. Rare as a first name, it occurs more commonly as a surname and is usually spelled Cleland or Clelland. "I think my dad loved the name, as unusual as it was," Michael said.[2]

William and Ina sold their house in August 1905, just two years after building it, realizing a profit of $259.61 on the transaction. The Cards also unloaded a number of their relatively new household items at the same time, taking a loss that more than offset the profit from the house. For the next year or so, they boarded in smaller quarters near downtown. It's not known why the family spent this period in reduced circumstances, but they may have been trying to save money for the down payment on their next house, because in the summer of 1906, the Card family again moved into a house of their own. The roomy, three-story frame house was located in a quiet neighborhood near Lake of the Isles. It would remain William and Ina's home for many years, and in it their boy would grow into a young man.

Clellan, nicknamed Clell or (when he was little) Clelly, was an uncommonly good-looking child. A thatch of thick dark hair framed his expressive moon face. His limpid brown eyes were equally capable of oozing grave sincerity or sparkling with mischievious delight. Friends invariably describe Clellan as handsome, perhaps a surprising description to those who know him only as the preposterous buffoon Axel.

Clell grew into a thoughtful

The young Clellan
(or one of the Little Rascals?)

 Have you tasted the grub – worm?

person with varied interests and an infectious sense of humor. He enjoyed people and was always ready to gab. Somewhat surprisingly, though, he formed few intimate friendships outside of his family. Elaine Hogan, who knew Clellan for more than forty years, noted, "I don't think that he had many friends, but those that he had were very close. He was just a wonderful friend."

Clellan grew up in a now-vanished world that today almost seems like some Victorian fairy tale. Many years later, he recalled some impressions of his youth in a column he wrote for a Minnetonka newspaper:

REMEMBER –

Big snowy winters and the wonderful sound of sleigh bells and the wonderful, squeaky noise of steel runners on the snow?

The man from the gas company, the lamplighter, with the flaming stick, who used to go from gas lamp-post to gas lamp-post, in the cities just before dusk – They even wrote a song about the lamplighters.

How your stomach ache would improve suddenly when grandma approached with a large spoonful of sulphur and molasses? Corset covers – teddy bears – bloomers – heavy underwear – sleeve garters – boiled shirts?!

Like many people living during the dawn of the automobile age, the young Clellan loved cars. His vehicles, from his first Ford flivver to his big Buick Roadmaster convertible, were prized possessions. A long drive on a beautiful day was his idea of a good time. In his newspaper column, many of his recollections centered on automobiles:

REMEMBER –

The advent of demountable rims for autos? Ah! What a step forward!

When the dispenser of gasoline used a large funnel, inside of which was stretched a piece of chamois-skin to strain out various small particles which were invariably found in gasoline of the "early days"?

When Dad always chose Sunday morning around 8 A.M. to tune up the motor on the old 40-horse touring car, because most of the day was spent in touring from the Twin Cities to Lake Minnetonka – and home again! An exhausting tour of 50 miles and two flat tires!!

I remember as a very small boy being tucked snugly between Mom and Dad in the front (and only) seat of our early model Ford roadster, and taking our regular Sunday outing on Park Avenue in Minneapolis. Of course anybody that had a vehicle in those days, either horse or motor propelled,

*would joy-ride Sunday afternoons on Park Avenue – the showcase of Min-
neapolis in those days. One thing that I remember very well is that all I
could see of the front of the little Ford roadster was the very tip-top of the
brass radiator cap. Another thing I remember is the sound on Sunday
afternoons on Park Avenue: the rhythmic clip-clop of the horses' hooves –
the well-groomed quadrupeds proudly drew fashionable carriages then,
and believe me, the horseless carriages were out-numbered (of course, that
was B.L. (Before Laramie [the Ford automobile dealer in Excelsior when
the article was written]).*

*In the 1912 to 1916 era (if I'm wrong, please drop me a note) garages
and used car dealers didn't exist to the extent they do today. Individuals
bought and sold cars among themselves – it was felt that you could really
take the word of an individual if he said his 1912 Cadillac only had so
many thousand miles on it.*

*I can hear my Dad now inquiring about an ad in the Sunday "Autos for
Sale" section of the Sunday Journal:*

"Does the car have electric or gas lights?"

"Demountable rims?"

"Four doors?"

"Left- or right-hand drive?"

"Will it go up Kenwood Hill (Minneapolis) on high?"

"Self starter?"

"One man top?"

"How many horse-power – 30 or 40?"

And so on and so on and so on!!!

*I remember a Winton Six my Dad was demonstrating to a prospective
customer one sunny Sunday afternoon and little Clellan was riding in the
back seat listening to my Dad expound the merits of this beautiful (and it
was) automobile. We approached the testing ground for all automobiles
of that era – Kenwood Hill! As Dad took quite a long run for the hill and
all six cylinders were laboring to the very limit of their 40 h.p., Dad took
another bite on his cigar, the prospective customer in the front seat next
to Dad took a better hold on his hat, little Clelly (me) leaned between Dad
and the customer and said, "If it goes up without shifting it'll be the first
time!" Well – Pop's neck got awful red but the old car made it (with the
aid of a few knocks and grunts) and the customer did buy the car, and little Clelly (that's me) didn't get his hide tanned after all.*

In about 1908, Clell began attending Douglas Elementary School
in Minneapolis where he soon showed an interest in performing.
The climax of this early phase of his career came on May 5, 1916, in
a citywide celebration commemorating the tercentenary of William

Clellan on one of his first vehicles

Shakespeare's death. Among the festivities was a performance of *Master Will of Stratford*, a play about the twelve-year-old Shakespeare, a boy "who believed in fairies and who delighted in weaving stories about all with whom he came in contact." In the melodrama, the young Will gets into trouble with the squire of a neighboring estate, and he appeals directly to Queen Elizabeth for justice. Later, in a dream, the boy finds himself in the middle of a dispute between Oberon and Titania, the fairy king and queen. All ends happily, of course; when he awakes, Will discovers that the fairies have given him a magic quill which will enable him to write his masterpieces.

Clellan was chosen for the title role, heading an all-star cast of more than 60 pupils selected from nine Minneapolis grade schools. The students developed their own interpretations of the characters, resulting in a "natural, unaffected performance." According to a newspaper report of the time, Clellan played the young Shakespeare as "something of a dreamer and with a suggestion of the poet though not so much as to make him other than a real boy."

At one point in the play, Will drives away a witch by chanting the alphabet in reverse. Clellan got a lot of mileage out of that bit. Forty years later, Axel impressed kids by reciting the alphabet backwards, a feat that he claimed "nobody else can do. You hafta be awful well-educated to do that, see, and have an open mind," he declared. "I got holes in my head! Ha-ha-ha!"

Years later, some wags claimed that Shakespeare had turned over in his grave the night Clellan performed as the Bard. It's true that the audience began to walk out before the play ended, but this wasn't due to any lack of talent on Clellan's part. The play was a lengthy three acts, and also included a prologue and an epilogue. When

What are we having for breakfast – my very good friend?

the curtain came down after the third act, with the epilogue still to come, the audience thought the performance was over and started to leave. The school principal had to make an unscheduled curtain call to plead with the crowd to stay. Despite the confusion, the student drama "found favor with the large audience of fathers, mothers, and 'the sisters and the cousins and the aunts' of the actors."

Like the character he had played, the adolescent Clellan was a bit of a romantic. Years later, he recounted one of the idle daydreams that occasionally occupied his thoughts in those halcyon days:

I remember the wonderful old street car boats that used to grace Lake Minnetonka; also the streetcars that used to transport people to and from the lake. Many people would spend a great part of the summer at the then popular "summer resorts" and rely upon the Twin Cities Rapid Transit company's networks of street car lines and streetcar boats to get them to and from their offices.

What a thrill I experienced as the big "Lake Minnetonka," "Tonka Bay," or "Deephaven" car would approach! I'd eagerly board it and try to get a front seat right near the motor-man so I could get a first-hand view of how he handled things. I took mental note of how the motor-man did every-thing but steer the thing: what made it move forward, what stopped the massive mass of steel, how he tooted the warning system, even the wob-bly slightly padded stool he sat on when tired [of] standing – oh yes, what handle he used to open the gates (there was only one entrance and exit on street cars in those days) at the rear of the car.

Like all kids I could close my eyes and imagine what would happen if the motor-man should faint while the car was plummeting down the steel rails at 65 miles per hour. I knew what I'd do, yes, I'd slide the door back which divided the passenger section from the motor-man's cab, I'd quickly apply the brakes (though gently – they were air brakes), bring the speed-ing monster within control, and call back for two strong passengers to carry the prostrate motor-man to the passenger section and make him as comfortable as possible while I summoned an ambulance at the next stop. Ah, such are the dreams of imaginative youth! Wasn't I silly?

Clellan at Blake School, about 1921

CHAPTER 2

AMONG THE ROSEBUDS AND CACTUS

IN THE FALL OF 1917 Clellan entered West High School in Minneapolis, where he proved to be a less-than-impressive pupil. By the end of that first year, he had passing marks in just two subjects: English and manual training. In spite of this underwhelming record, his parents somehow managed to get him admitted to prestigious Blake High School beginning in September of 1918. In order to qualify, however, Clellan had to take special instruction in Latin and algebra during the summer. He "worked faithfully" but somehow he never quite got around to taking examinations in either subject before school began.

A private school for boys, Blake catered primarily to the well-to-do, but its aim was to teach that "wealth means responsibility rather than privilege." The campus was in the Minneapolis suburb of Hopkins on five acres of tree-lined hills; at that time, the grounds were surrounded only by a few scattered farms. Students and teachers at Blake were encouraged to use the Twin Cities' extensive trolley system to get to the remote campus, rather than drive autos. It was all part and parcel of the notion that Blake students shouldn't have any more privileges than did the average Joe.

Although his only valid credit from West High was in English, the young Card was enrolled as a sophomore at Blake. In contrast to the 140 freshmen at West, Clellan's new class consisted of fewer than twenty students. He made the second string of Blake's football squad, too, which from Clell's perspective may well have been the most important thing; he loved football passionately.

 Gramma lost her stocking – darner!

No sooner had he gotten settled at his new school when all classes were cancelled indefinitely due to the worldwide influenza epidemic. A member of Blake's faculty and one student died, and millions more perished around the world. Death also struck the Card family during this period as Clellan lost both of his grandfathers in little more than a month: Isaac Card was fatally injured in an accident on August 31, 1918, and Ira Covey died on October 9.

On November 18, it was finally deemed safe to reopen the school, but Blake's demanding curriculum soon had Clellan struggling. Dr. Card doubtless had hoped that his son would replicate his own successful school career but "like father, like son" definitely did not apply in matters of academia. Clellan had difficulty attaining even average marks, although he certainly wasn't stupid. One of his instructors described Clellan as "a boy with mercurial disposition. Arouse his ambition and belief in himself, and he does very satisfactory work."

Nevertheless, Dr. Card became understandably concerned about his son's poor performance and questioned whether the school's standards were perhaps too high. Blake's principal somewhat testily responded, "I am sure you feel that standards in medicine, in dentistry, in business, must be high, and that high standards won with an effort are better than lower standards won with comparative ease."

If anyone had asked Clellan, he might have said that he'd prefer easier, lower standards. In his first year at Blake, Clellan failed English, history, and algebra. He took make-up exams and failed those as well. Thanks to intensive individual instruction, he barely passed Latin. The following fall, Clell advanced to the junior class anyway, the headmaster optimistically believing that he could still catch up. Clellan did show promise in some ways: he was elected the president of the junior class and a junior member of the senior council. He also was selected as the assistant advertising manager for the 1920 edition of *The Callopan*, the school yearbook.

And of course, there was football. As a junior, Clellan made the first string football team – and then Blake proceeded to lose the first three games of the season. In the fourth, against Wayzata, Clell got his big chance. On the very first play of the second quarter, he ran fifty-five yards for a touchdown. He went on to make two more touch-

Say, Garbo, what are you going to do with your double – boiler?

downs, the only scores of the game, winning the contest for Blake 18–0. He continued to play outstanding football for the rest of the 1919 season. That December Clellan was awarded the coveted school letter, which he wore with great pride.

Clellan was also getting noticed in school plays. On April 10, 1920, he appeared as The Friend in Dunsany's satire *Fame and the Poet*. His performance was called "excellent" and "a real characterization." One reviewer wrote that "the young actor had ease of stage presence to be envied by many an older toiler before the footlights." Another claimed that Clellan "did more to get the piece across than anyone else."

Clellan wearing his Blake letter sweater

Unfortunately, he still was not getting rave reviews for his academic performance. He'd been permitted to go on to junior English "on trial" and managed to pass. However, despite continued private tutoring, he only attained partial credit in Latin. Worse, he failed both plane geometry and Spanish. These results were so disappointing that the Cards seriously considered returning Clellan to West High School, where the standards weren't quite so high. Clellan himself probably convinced them to let him continue at Blake, all his difficulties notwithstanding, because he truly enjoyed attending school there. He stayed, but had to repeat his junior year.

Just before the school year began, on the morning of September 6, 1920, Clellan and seven other fellows (later joined by four more) left Minneapolis, probably travelling by train. Their destination was Blake Camp, a rustic collection of cabins on the shore of Lake Hubert, 150 miles north of the Twin Cities. The school had operated the camp for about a year, offering students an opportunity to experience the great outdoors each summer. That year, after the regular season had ended, something new was being tried: football camp. The idea was to conduct intensive pre-season training to give Blake's team an edge over its opponents.

Tucked among the evergreen trees, the camp overlooked Lake Hubert from a sandy bluff. The compound consisted of one main house and six oblong chalets, each sleeping up to four people. During the first few days, training was comparatively light. Even so, on the afternoon the boys arrived, practice started as soon as everyone was settled.

The day's activities followed a regular schedule: a whistle blew at seven-thirty each morning and everyone took a quick, chilly dip in the lake. After breakfast, there generally was a five- to eight-mile hike around the lake, or a short practice. The boys spent the remainder of the morning writing letters, reading, or playing cards. Lunch was the big meal of the day, and the camp offered "none but the healthiest food." Another short rest period followed the meal, and then at three o'clock came the main event: two hours of exhausting football practice. When the boys finished, they usually went swimming or canoeing to cool off. After supper, they often played baseball or other games until dark. In the evenings, they gathered around the birchlog mantle of the fireplace in the main house where the camp's Victrola cranked out music until everyone was ready for bed, usually by nine o'clock. After ten days of this strenuous routine, the Blake football team returned to Minneapolis – in shape, invigorated, and intent on winning.

That golden autumn of 1920, win they did. In their first game on October 12, they gained a decisive 28–0 victory against West High School. Their next opponents were outclassed completely, as Blake steamrollered Hopkins 68–0. In a critical contest with St. Thomas, with the field in a "flood of water," Clellan and his teammates again triumphed, 14–7. Another rout ensued when Blake crushed Wayzata 70–0. In the next game, penalties totalling 120 yards failed to stop the Blake juggernaut and the team handily beat University High, 28–0.

On Friday November 12, Blake met its traditional rival, St. Paul Academy, for the final game of the season. Winter was in the air, and a snowy wind blew across the frozen playing field. Neither school was able to score in the first half, but Blake suffered a severe blow

Where did you get the green garter – snake?

tinued offering humorous bits to the *Blake Torch*. He helped plan
the junior–senior dance, and "the affair moved with almost uncon-
ceivable smoothness." In January 1922, he also attended the senior–
junior party, which did not move quite as smoothly. The kids
journeyed to the school for skating and sliding, but a blizzard put
an end to outdoor fun. Carried indoors, the remainder of the party
went well until it was time to go home. In the cold and snow, nearly
every car had trouble starting or got stuck. Late that night, after driving some friends home, Clellan's auto collided with a taxicab on the
slippery streets. He was knocked unconscious and taken to Hillcrest
Hospital, where he woke up badly bruised but otherwise fine.

Clellan also continued his thespian career, appearing in the farce
Bills on April 8, but he received his first critical review. Although one
reviewer wrote that "Card has an enviable poise," another took him
to task: "Card was good, but some hard work on the part would have
made him much better. He was distinctly below his ability. He should
not neutralize genuine talent by careless reading of lines, and a general impression of eleventh-hour preparation." Considering Clellan's
ongoing scholastic struggles, it may well be that the reviewer was
correct about his lack of readiness.

Clell's edition of *The Callopan* in 1922 would have provided a fitting cap to his high school career – if only he had graduated that
year. His name popped up everywhere on its pages. In addition to
editing the yearbook, he did a clutch of crudely drawn but amusing
cartoons for it. He was again voted "Best Football Player," and he was
also named "Handsomest," "Loudest," "Big-
gest Bluffer," and "Most Modest." He placed
second or third in "Best Athlete," "Biggest
Fusser," "Longest Winded," "Most Reck-
less," "Best Dancer," "Most Gentlemanly,"
and paradoxically, "Most Villainous." In
total, Clellan charted in twelve categories,
more than any other student. He was even
credited with instituting a fad of wearing
golfing trousers, which in one of his cartoons he extolled as "the gnat's nostrils"
(parodying the then-current phrase "the
bee's knees").

Clellan in the 1922 edition of
The Callopan

Clellan's popularity at school was a harbinger of things to come. His ease in front of a camera is already evident in some of the yearbook photographs, and he had grown into quite a good-looking young man. In his senior photo, his thick shock of brown hair slicked back, his mouth set in determination above the firm line of his chin, a puckish glint in his eyes, he could have been the prototype of "Jack Armstrong, the All-American Boy." The portentous aphorism below his picture read, "Men, like bullets, go farthest when they are smoothest."

Unfortunately, his energy and charm were of no avail in his classes. By the end of the school year in June, Clell had again failed three subjects, and he'd dropped two others in the middle of the year. These results were so abysmal that the headmaster changed his mind about Clellan. He wrote to Dr. Card again, and began by apologizing:

"I am very sorry that you must suffer the disappointment in looking at the enclosed report card. It is very difficult to give advice in this case. But it seems to me that I owe you the utmost frankness in discussing Clellan's future best interests.

"I believe that he had better go to work. The good qualities will be better developed in doing what is congenial whereas they are stunted, I fear, in continuing work in which he is not interested."

It seemed out of the question for Clellan to ever graduate from Blake, especially since the school's headmaster had finally given up on him. His parents, however, would not. In the autumn of 1922, Clell was enrolled in West High School again. He immediately tried out for the West High football team, and promptly got injured. One late September afternoon, Clell showed up at Blake on crutches to forlornly watch his former teammates practice.

The dizzying array of extracurricular activities Clellan had enjoyed at Blake was sharply curtailed at West High; he obviously needed to concentrate on his schoolwork. The lure of the stage proved too strong to ignore, though. Clell joined the Dramatic Club and in November 1922, appeared in the play *The Loving Cup*. Despite keeping a relatively low profile at West High, Clell was voted "Handsomest Boy" of his class (along with two others). His senior picture in the 1923 edition of *The Hesperian*, the West High yearbook, again shows why. His head cocked slightly to one side, Clellan stares at

Clellan's college portrait

sions, re-examinations, and low grades. Worse, this time there was no sympathetic headmaster to give him a break. By the fall of 1924, he had so much work to make up that he had to forgo playing football. Midway through his sophomore year, Clellan acknowledged to his parents that he had flunked two classes, eked out a D minus in another, and got Cs in three more. He achieved Bs in just two classes: physical training and public speaking. It was a clear indication of where his real interests lay.

Clellan's college letters home provide clues about the nature of his problem with school. "The exams are going on this week and I am doing too much worrying I guess because I have been sort of disgusted with myself. I go to the exam feeling that I know the stuff pretty well and when the thing is put before me my brain ceases to function. I have put just as much time on my work as anybody else, have had no outside attractions and get along alright from day to day, then the exams come along and I go to pieces on them."

One of his professors told Clellan that he hadn't learned how to take exams yet. "He said that is why I did poorly, because I ended the exam hour about 3/4 thru with my exam. That is true with all my exams." In another letter he wrote, "Every time I start thinking of exams starting the 29th my stomach gets sick!" As finals approached one spring, his nervousness even caused physical problems.

His dreams were haunted, too: "I had the damnedest time trying to get to sleep last night. All I could think of was exams – professors – flunking out – and when I did get to sleep I dreamed about them – and I woke up in a cold sweat." It seems likely that Clellan suffered from what today would be called test anxiety.

Far worse than any academic trials, Clellan missed Marion terribly. The two of them had been one thousand miles apart for the better part of two years. Perhaps he couldn't stand to be separated from Marion any longer, or maybe he simply had to face the stark reality of his scholastic record. Whatever the reason, on January 30, 1926, Clellan officially withdrew from Rutgers, well short of a diploma. The ostensible reason was "to enter the School of Business at the University of Minn." But he never did.

Later, during his broadcasting career, "authorized" biographies of Clellan often erroneously claimed that he was a college graduate. Since his public image was that of a corn-prone jokester, it may be that station management wanted to coat his hick persona with the veneer of a college man, lest people get the impression that Clellan was a genuine hayseed. There's no evidence that Clellan himself lied about having earned a diploma; in fact, in interviews he always simply said that he "attended" Rutgers, which was perfectly true. However, the false claim turns up again and again over the course of his career, and even close associates such as Mary Davies believed that he had graduated, so evidently he didn't try very hard to correct the misinformation either.[4]

When the young Card returned to Minneapolis in early 1926, he faced the problem of making a living. He quickly landed his first job, finding employment as a life insurance salesman for the White & Odell Agency. After managing to sell a policy to himself, he found

What did the chicken do when it cracked open its shell, li'l Bo – peep?

few other good prospects. Ten months of effort yielded little more than gas money to show for it, so Clellan abandoned the insurance game for a job as a service station attendant for the Standard Oil Company. Always a go-getter, Clellan worked hard and eventually got a position on the company's sales force.

His sales career with the oil company got off to a promising start, but Clellan wasn't satisfied. He wanted a faster route to the top. In 1927, the young eager beaver began a new career as a bond salesman at the First Minneapolis Trust Company in downtown Minneapolis. Within a year, he joined George M. Forman & Company, an investment securities firm in the Metropolitan Bank Building. Years later, Clellan (as Axel) recalled, "I worked in a bank one time when I was but a mere sapling. I was the draft clerk in the bank where I worked. I opened and shut the windows every morning and night. I was really quite a help around the joint."

Clellan and Marion in the 1920s

Clellan's engaging personality and ready wit were definite assets in selling bonds, and he appeared to be well on the way to success. It seemed to be an opportune time to propose marriage to Marion, and she happily consented. The one condition (dictated by Marion's doctrinaire Catholic mother) was that Clellan convert to Catholicism. Though born a Presbyterian, Clellan nonetheless readily assented and he became a faithful practitioner of his adopted religion. In fact, his mother Ina also was baptised a Catholic on her deathbed.

The wedding took place on Wednesday morning, October 10, 1928, in the Church of St. Thomas the Apostle. It was a notable social event, attended by more than 300 people. The mood was set by a string quartet from the Minneapolis Symphony Orchestra performing a variety of classical pieces. The altar, festooned with innumer-

Part of the wedding party (L to R: Best man William Card, Clellan, and Marion;
Elaine Hogan is on the far right)

able palms, cybotium ferns, and baskets of giant chrysanthemums, was lit by white cathedral candles flickering in branched candelabra. The bridesmaids were attired in dresses of eggshell yellow satin and drooping, wide-brimmed hats of violet velvet. Marion wore a gown of ivory transparent velvet, while the groom sweated it out in a dark tuxedo.

Clellan had selected his father to be his best man, a most unusual choice even in those days, but a testament to the close relationship between father and son. His dad truly was his best friend. Clellan put his feelings succinctly when he inscribed a photo portrait, "To my Dad – The greatest guy in the world." A small reception at 510 Groveland Avenue followed the ceremony. Immediately afterwards, the newlyweds left for their honeymoon in New York City and Washington, D.C.

Upon their return to Minneapolis, Clellan and Marion set up housekeeping in an apartment just down the street from Clellan's parents. At first, everything was rosy. The young marrieds were very much in love, and Clellan was doing fine as a bond salesman. Their happiness seemed complete when, on July 10, 1929, their first son,

 What did you do when you seen your wife sittin' in the china – clipper?

Clellan Peter Card, was born. (The family joke was that Peter was born nine months and ten minutes after the wedding ceremony.)

All was not well in paradise, however. The Roaring Twenties were about to come to a screeching halt as they crashed into the Great Depression, and Clellan's career would be one of the many casualties. It may be that his heart wasn't in his work, anyway. There's a tale told about an evening when Clellan and Marion planned to have a few guests over for cocktails. Prohibition was still in force, so providing alcoholic refreshments could be a bit of a problem, but Clellan was resourceful. As the story goes, the fete was fated to take place on the day that the stock market crashed. On that black October day, most brokers were frantically trying to sell their clients' stocks and bonds. Clellan, blissfully unaware of the chaos, was running all over town trying to get enough bootleg gin for his party!

Clellan's job at George M. Forman & Company soon evaporated as the organization went bankrupt. He then became a bond salesman for the Mann Securities Company but within a year that job also vanished. The nimble Clellan moved on to yet another investment firm, G. E. Barrett & Company, but that company soon met its end as well. By then, there seemed to be no future in selling bonds at all.

With a family to support and jobs almost nonexistent, a desperate Clellan became a door-to-door salesman. He tried peddling everything from refrigerators to brushes – anything to make a little cash. But even the considerable Card charm couldn't sell merchandise to customers with no money. It wasn't long before Clellan, too, was completely and utterly broke.

Things got so bad that the elder Cards finally had to lend a helping hand. Clell's disconsolate young family moved out of their tiny apartment and into the haven of his boyhood home. Clellan was right back where he had started, and the future looked bleak.

Clellan Card
The One Clown, Multivoiced Show

Who broadcasts Northrup, King & Co's "Almanac of The Air" over WCCO every week day morning starting at 7:00 o'clock

A postcard mailed to Clellan's radio fans in early 1937. The stuffed animal Clellan's holding may represent one of his sidekicks, Mahitabel or Noggins.

CHAPTER 4

DiPP!NG INTo THE AiRWAVES

RADIO IS SO COMMONPLACE TODAY, perhaps even outmoded, that it's difficult now to appreciate how exciting and enthralling it once was. World War I spurred technical advancements that ultimately made possible the new concept of "broadcasting": transmitting an audio signal from a single location to multiple receivers in many different places. By the early 1920s, radio was ready to begin its conquest of the world.

Small radio stations, most of them 250 watts or less, sprang up in cities across the United States. One such pioneer station was WLAG in Minneapolis, which first went on the air in 1922 but was soon struggling financially. On October 2, 1924, it became WCCO radio, named for Washburn Crosby Company, the business that had come to the moribund station's rescue.

On March 4, 1925, WCCO dedicated new studios on the twelfth and thirteenth floors of the one-year-old Nicollet Hotel, located at the confluence of Washington, Nicollet, and Hennepin Avenues in downtown Minneapolis. The brand-new studios, described as "sumptuous" and "modern," were state of the art at the time.

By 1929, WCCO had been selected as one of forty "clear channel" radio stations in the United States, which meant that no other station anywhere in the country was permitted to operate on WCCO's designated frequency after sundown. To take full advantage of this privilege, an incredibly powerful 50,000 watt transmitter was constructed in Anoka. The station's primary audience – those living within 200

 How'd you like to go fishing with a broad – Castor?

The Nicollet Hotel

miles of the transmitter – was estimated to be a potential 4,100,000 people, tuned in to approximately 400,000 radios (ten people per radio!). WCCO radio was well on its way to becoming a broadcasting giant.

At about this time, in the spring of 1930, William Card gave a series of talks on WCCO. The underemployed Clellan sometimes accompanied his dad to the radio station and got to know a few members of the staff. One day, someone at the studio asked him if his voice was as good as his father's. Clell replied in his most mellifluous tones that it was, and got an audition. Shortly after, the station called Clellan to do a bit part in a program sponsored by a rod and reel manufacturer. He played the role of Izaak Walton, the famed seventeenth-century fisherman and author of *The Compleat Angler*. Clell was paid the princely sum of $4.50 for his efforts. He immediately splurged and spent his entire wage – on food for his family.

Over the next few months, Clellan continued to work occasionally around the WCCO studios, doing bit parts and odd jobs. He liked working in the still-young field of radio; in fact, he enjoyed it so much that he never really considered it to be work. With two other mouths to feed and no home to call his own, though, Clellan needed a steady job. He began to look around for other opportunities in the radio business. He found a niche at station WDGY. In comparison to the colossus that WCCO was already becoming, the other radio stations in the Twin Cities were small potatoes. WDGY in particular was a shoestring operation: a maverick, marginal studio owned by an eccentric jeweler-optometrist named Dr. George Young.

Dr. Young was a dapper gent with a penchant for loud clothes and conspicuous diamonds. The flamboyant doctor was particularly skilled at self-promotion; in front of his store, his name was set into the sidewalk in brass letters, and billboards advertising his businesses often featured large pictures of him. He also loved

What did you do when your boyfriend went to the party with B.O.- plenty?

CHAPTER 5

AXEL AND HIS ... HOG?

AXEL'S HEYDAY ON TELEVISION was during the 1950s and 1960s but he first lurched into the public consciousness on radio. In fact, his origins went all the way back to the early decades of the twentieth century. Sometime between 1916 and 1920, Clellan's parents hired a young housekeeper named Nellie Johnson, who had recently emigrated from Sweden. She made a lasting impression on the adolescent Clellan, or at least her voice did. He became fascinated by her accent and learned to mimic it perfectly. Clellan's shtick as a Nordic hick later became the foundation of his career, although there was nary a drop of Scandinavian blood in the Card family.[5]

Clellan had been getting laughs with his Swede routine since high school, but his radio gig gave him the opportunity to flesh out a whole character. He created a daffy Norseman, a Swedish meathead who took demented delight in atrocious puns and ancient jokes. Clellan christened his Scandinavian scalawag "Axel."

At 8:30 A.M. on Thursday, February 18, 1937, WCCO announcer Max Karl introduced Axel to the radio audience. The comedic character made his debut on, of all things, a "news" show entitled *Axel the Newscaster*. The first ads for the show don't even mention the name of Clellan Card, although there's no doubt that he starred as Axel. His true identity may not have been revealed to the radio audience immediately in order to generate interest in the character. Axel delivered humorous news reports in his inimitable style: heavily-accented English, laced with puns and malapropisms. The production also may have "dramatized" the news with a variety of sound effects.[6]

The Swedish anchorman had a co-star equal to the *savoir farce* of

 Hey, they tell me your new car is shot in the rear – Axel!

the show; Axel's first partner was a pig named Suey. Just what the swine did on the program isn't known, but perhaps he delivered an occasional editorial "oink." In addition to news spoofs and porcine snorts, the fifteen-minute show also included "favorite melodies." Besides doing the radio show, Axel and his hog made a number of personal appearances for the Red Owl food stores, the program's sponsor. The two hams performed at Red Owl dealers' meetings and other promotional gatherings. Unfortunately, there are no known photographs of Clellan attired in the costume or make-up that he may have used for these appearances.

Axel the Newscaster lasted for only three months, airing for the final time on May 28, 1937. The character, however, proved to be more durable. WCCO's programming director, Hayle C. Cavanor, thought that Axel was funnier than Clellan's *Almanac* character Pops. It was an opinion that carried considerable weight. Cavanor was a shrewd and respected manager who had risen from the ranks of the sales department and whose instincts had helped make WCCO radio a tremendous success. Cavanor's own career was also a testament to the progressive leadership that the station enjoyed. In an era when executives were almost exclusively male, Cavanor – the head of programming at one of the country's highest-rated radio stations – was a woman. With her encouragement, Clellan made his Norse nitwit a part of the *Almanac of the Air* show, and by 1939 Axel had become the show's main character.

Hayle C. Cavanor

A promotional release touting Clellan's services that year breathlessly proclaimed:

In his Swedish characterization of Axel, which ran commercially for some time over WCCO, Clellan Card established a personality as real as Charlie McCarthy. Axel and his pig have been in constant demand for personal appearances, and never fail to steal the show. Axel's influence has been felt in high places and low, among old and young. In the Minneapolis high schools, instructors in Swed-

I thought you was on the boat – doc!

CHAPTER 6

THE MORNING
MIRTHQUAKE

NORTHRUP, KING'S ORIGINAL PLAN was to sponsor *Almanac of the Air* for a single season, until mid-June of 1937. By the spring of that year, however, the program had become hugely popular, especially in rural areas. Some dairymen even put radios in their barns so that they could listen to Clellan milking gags while they were milking cows. Northrup, King definitely had a hit on their hands, so the run of *Almanac of the Air* was extended indefinitely.

Dubbed "the Morning Mirthquake" by fellow WCCO personality Cedric Adams, Clellan soon developed a running gag about serving coffee and doughnuts to the members of the studio audience. He would invite his listeners to "come on up and dunk a sinker with us some morning." Anyone gullible enough to take him up on the offer discovered that it was just a jest; the refreshments were fictitious. Very few complained, however, because those early risers who made the trek to the studio could stay to watch the live broadcast, which in those days was quite a treat in itself. As many as fifteen or twenty fans a day had shown up at the radio studio even before Clell began encouraging people to come. After he began issuing his invitation to the dunk, the tally rose to 85, 100, even 150 people in the studio audience – day in, day out.

As his popularity grew, Clellan was tapped for more and more radio shows. On February 3, 1937, Clellan joined the afternoon program *Ladies First*, providing comedy relief. One of the other featured performers on the show, and often the butt of Clellan's jibes, was

 What did you do after you ate the meat – loaf?

Clellan welcoming guests to *Almanac of the Air*

rotund piano player Toby Prin. A talented musician, composer, and natural entertainer, the jovial Toby was born in Ishpeming, Michigan, "on an undisclosed date." He began his career as "Tiny Speck," fronting a band in the Virginia–Eveleth area of northern Minnesota. He moved to Minneapolis in 1934 and signed with WCCO almost immediately. Playing solo, with small combos, or in large orchestras, he was a fixture on Twin Cities broadcasting for the next quarter-century. He and Clellan became good friends and worked together often over the years.

In the spring of 1937, Clellan also became the host of *Meet the Missus*. The format of this afternoon program was apparently syndicated to other radio markets such as Chicago, Cleveland, and Detroit. The Minneapolis version featured Clellan bantering with women, live from Miller's Cafeteria. Clell's relaxed manner and way with a wisecrack made him adept at this sort of informal interview, and he would do many such shows in the years to come.

Clellan found himself in demand for public appearances, too. As early as March 1937, Northrup, King began to utilize him as a speaker at some of their sales meetings and company functions. Over

What did you get for your birthday, Bobby – socks?

The Night Before Christmas

**A Parody Done in Swedish Dialect by Clellan Card on the
Northrup, King & Co's. Christmas Program
December 23, 1938**

It vas de night before Xmas, ven all tru de place
vere ay vas staying

Dere vasn't nobody making no noise, not eefen
som mouses except my brudder-in-law and
he is a rat.

De stockings vere hanged by de shimney kinda
careful

Because dat feller vit de red knickers vas supposed to be dere.

De little shavers vas all snug in dere beds

Vile visions of sugar plums vas dancing in dere
heads

And mama in her curlers and ay in my night
shirt

Had yust vashed our feet for a long vinter's nap.

Ven out on de Northrup, King lawn dere arose
a heck of a noise

Ay yumped out of may bed to see if it vas de
boys,

Avay to de vindow ay flew like a flash

Ay coulda made it faster but ay'd yust ate some
hash.

De Moon vas shining on de new Snow wot had
yust come down

And it vas kinda shining like it vasn't night

And vat to my vondering eyes should appear

But a little teeney-weeney sleigh and eight tiny
horses.

Dere vas a tiny little driver — so sudden and
quick

Ay could tell right avay in may night shirt it
was yolly St. Nick

More faster dan eagles his horses dey came

And he whistled and hollered and called em
bad names.

Now hasher—now trasher—now vixer—now
prancer

On Cosmetics—On Stupid—On Visconsin—On
Pittsburg

To de top of de porch to de top of de vall

Now pass avay, pass avay, pass out for cat's
sake!

And in two shakes of a skunk's tail ay heard on
de roof

Dose animals monkeying around mit dere feet

As ay sucked in may head and tripped over
de cat

Down de shimney came Santa Claus flat on his
back.

He vas fat as a old hog—right yolly old elf

And ay laughed ven ay seen him—ay couldn't
help it.

A vink of his eye and a twist of his head

Soon gave me to know ay didn't have nothin
to vorry about.

Vat vas left of his pipe he held in his tooth

And de smoke wrapped around his head like
a hoop.

He was qvite broad in places—he had a round
little belly

Dat shook ven he'd snicker—like a bottle of
likker.

His eyes dey vas glassy—his suit vas de berries,

His cheeks vas like roses—his nose like some
Cherries

His droll little mouth vas drawed up like a bow

And de beard on his chin dragged down in de
snow.

He didn't say nothin—but vent straight to his
verk

And put lots of pretty stuff in de hosiery and
turned vit a squirt

And putting his fingers in front of his nose

He says—"You know me Kids" and, holy
smoke! he vas gone.

He yumped in his big open yob, and to his team
gave a vistle he had promised em for
Christmas

And dey yumped up and ran like dey had sat
on some tistles

Ay heard him say as he scrammed out of dere

"A Snappy Christmas to all and to all—Ay hope
yu get vat yu vant."

Listen to Northrup, King & Co.'s Radio Program on WCCO every week-day morning at 7:00

planned. Unlike the year before, this time the station anticipated a
large crowd, so the station took the precaution of reserving the grand
ballroom of the Nicollet Hotel, where only ticket-holders would be
admitted. By Tuesday, March 21, just three days after the first men-

tion, a flood of telephone and mail requests had exhausted the ticket supply. Clellan told his listeners that the special show had sold out but requests continued to come in anyway. By the end of March some 3,800 applications for tickets had been tallied, enough to fill the ballroom nearly three times over.

The devotion of some of Clellan's fans could be measured out in miles. Two couples from Lake Wilson, a small town in southwestern Minnesota, arose at 2:00 A.M. on that chilly April Fools' morning. Sleepy but full of anticipation, they drove 230 miles through the early morning darkness to the Twin Cities – just to dunk doughnuts with Clellan Card. A few hundred listeners made similar trips from other distant points.

Local fans, too, had to wake early to get in on the fun; the competition for seating was fierce. One of the first arrivals was the show's champion joke submitter, an 83-year-old female fan who listened to *Almanac of the Air* every day. The mayor of Minneapolis, George E.

At the Doughnut Dunking Jamboree, Clellan liked his doughnuts super-sized!

  What did you do when you didn't find any gold – fish?

Leach, arrived on the scene at 6:05 A.M. to find 300 people already there ahead of him. By 6:30 almost all the seats in the ballroom were taken, and by 6:45 the hall had filled, with several hundred more people packed into the standing room at the back. At 6:50 the standing room was exhausted, and the doors were closed. By showtime, an estimated

One of the coffee oases at the 1939 Donut Dunking Jamboree

1,800 folks, an unprecedented crowd for a local morning radio program, were squeezed into the hall.

At 7:00 A.M., the show opened as usual, with the sound of a cuckoo clock – but the bird cuckooed eleven times. (It was April Fools' Day, after all.) Clellan was in fine form, filling the air with wisecracks and jokes, and adopting a parade of voices as he acted out various character parts in his stories. News, weather, and music were interspersed as usual throughout the half-hour. Highlights of the proceedings included a dunking contest between two Minneapolis Fire Department captains and two police officers, each wielding a giant doughnut, and a remarkable ritual initiating Minneapolis Mayor Leach into the "Society of Donut Dunkers of America." Florence Lehman, the popular star of WCCO's *Ladies First* and *Talk of the Town*, also made a guest appearance.

After the broadcast, the crowd descended on the many "oases" of Chocolate Cream Coffee set up at strategic points around the Nicollet Hotel Ballroom and Mezzanine Lounge. There they sharpened their own doughnut dunking skills until the supply of sinkers and java was exhausted. Everyone agreed that the Second Annual Doughnut Dunking Jamboree had been a spectacular success. It also had provided tangible proof of Clellan's following. An informal survey of Minnesota State Fair visitors in 1938 had indicated that he was WCCO's most popular personality, ahead of even the celebrated Cedric Adams. By 1939, it was clear that Clellan Card was the biggest star on the biggest radio station in the entire upper Midwest.

Radio is an eggs-acting business!

CHAPTER 7

THe WORKING GIRL's FRIEND

"DID YOU HEAR CARD this morning?" became a familiar refrain in homes, offices, and stores throughout the upper Midwest. His popularity reached such proportions that even the networks became interested; CBS always kept its eye open for new talent with audience-grabbing potential, and Clellan Card must have sounded like a good prospect.

Northrop "Bun" Dawson, Jr., a writer and producer at WCCO radio in the early 1940s, recollected how "periodically, some of the 'big' CBS network shows would come out to the affiliates on tour, or for special events like the Aquatennial, and broadcast from the local affiliate studios like WCCO. Occasionally, they would enlist a local announcer to do the commercials. Clell did this on several occasions, as I recall, and did such a notable job that CBS offered him a position as a network announcer out of New York."

It never happened. Clellan simply had no desire to join the increasingly competitive radio rat race in New York, and was understandably concerned about the quality of life that his growing family would find there. An only child, he also was reluctant to move so far away from his parents. Besides, he probably felt that he already had it made. Dawson observed that Clellan's "roots were deep in Minnesota – his family, his friends, his loyal following." He was successful in a career he loved, in a city he loved, surrounded by people he loved – why should he leave?

WCCO radio naturally wanted to capitalize on Clellan's appeal, so the station continued to present him on various new shows. On May 13, 1939, the musical variety program *Saturday Morning Open House* premiered. Clellan and Eddie Gallaher were the announcers of the show, presented before a large studio audience in WCCO's fourth floor auditorium. *Open House* also featured a "galaxy of talent" that included a 12-piece orchestra conducted by violinist Wally Olson; the Harmonica Twins, Eddie and Tom Plehal; a group called the Ad Lib Club; a male octet under the direction of Ernie Garven; Harry Habata and his "rhythmical" accordion; vocalist Jeannie Arland or Flo Seidel; Kenny Spears on electric steel guitar; and "265 pound, jolly Toby Prin, who sings and composes with equal ease. Tubby Toby plays the piano on *Saturday Morning Open House* [and] plays with little Tommy, his son, on other mornings at his own house." In addition to this large roster of staff musicians, each week the best new talent was introduced to the radio audience as well.

It might seem that music alone could fill the three-quarters of an hour devoted to *Open House* each Saturday, but two ten-minute segments of every program featured something with even more allure: the "Kitchen Quiz." Hayle C. Cavanor (avowed expert in home economics, besides being WCCO's program director) acted as "the Quizmistress of the Air," while Clellan and his co-announcer took their mikes into the audience and selected contestants. Ms. Cavanor

A broadcast of *Saturday Morning Open House* in 1944 in WCCO's fourth-floor auditorium. Clellan is interviewing a woman in front of the stage on the left.

read questions pertaining to cooking or the kitchen, and prizes for a correct answer ranged from fifty cents all the way up to the queenly sum of five dollars. Losers were consoled with samples of a sponsor's product.

The "Kitchen Quiz" proved to be amazingly popular. Over the first two years of the program, mail for that segment of the show averaged 900 pieces a week. A telephone survey conducted on January 7, 1941, found that 40% of all radios in use were tuned to *Open House*, while only 17.6% were tuned to the second-ranked station. Within three years of the program's inception, WCCO could boast that one-and-a-half million people had sent in recipes or quiz questions, 50,000 women had attended the broadcasts, and more than $4,000 in prize money had been given away.

On July 24, 1939, Clellan and Marion's third and last child was born, named Michael Satterlee Card. That September, the Card clan moved to a new home at 4814 Colfax Avenue in the Southwest neighborhood of Minneapolis. A spacious, two-story abode that included an attic and finished basement as well, their new digs had plenty of room for the whole family. Clellan and Marion would spend nearly twenty years there.

Most of those years were happy ones. Clellan's mischievous sense of humor was always percolating. He might call a happily married friend late in the evening and say, "Polly, do you still wake up at night screaming for me?" Marion wasn't fazed by such antics, though. She told Bob DeHaven years later, "I knew I had his daily love, so it didn't bother me at all."

Mealtime in particular seemed to bring out the jester in Clell. At dinner, he might serve mashed potatoes by tossing them high into the air, then catch them on the plate in his hand. For Marion's thirty-fourth birthday, he presented her with a cake aglow with sixty-five candles. A magazine article described the atmosphere at the house of Cards this way:

> *Off the air or on, Clellan is the same guy – always ready with a quip for any occasion. In personal appearances, he's taken his share of heckling as every performer has. But the only time he's ever topped on a gag is at home where every meal turns into a "Can You Top This?" performance. His boys – Peter, 15; Johnny 10; and even Michael, 5 1/2 – are the stars and "Mommy" the admiring audience.*

What do you do with your excess – fat?

Peter, John, and Michael Card in about 1942

Elaine Hogan, Marion's friend since childhood and a bridesmaid at her wedding, was a frequent visitor. "It was more fun to be at their house and to be at the dinner table," she said, "because the repartee was just constant." Clellan and Marion proved to be stalwart friends as well, putting up Elaine at their house for three months in the aftermath of her mother's death. "It was so typical of Clellan," she said. "He was so good to everybody."

Clellan and Marion loved to entertain in their home, and had a reputation for throwing great parties. "Marion was a marvelous hostess," Elaine declared. "She was shy in a way but when she was on her home ground, she was very outgoing. She drew people out." During the shindigs, Clellan would often invite his guests downstairs to the basement amusement room to ask them to put their signatures on a wood-paneled support pillar there. As the years went on, the four faces of the pillar became crowded with names.

When the Card boys began to date girls, their parents occasionally hosted dinner parties for them. The teens, all dressed up for the big evening, were met at the house by Clellan playing the waiter. "We kind of knew what was coming, but with Clellan you never knew what the hell was gonna be next," laughed family friend Chuck Stanek. "He'd be dressed up in his soup-and-fish, and sometimes he'd put a mustache on himself, and he would have the towel over his arm, and he'd serve the dinner. He'd be very clumsy, and – 'Whoops!' – almost spill on one of the girls, and she'd shriek, you know."

At the end of the meal, Clellan would ask who wanted coffee. "Well, we were all very sophisticated in those days, and so we all wanted coffee, of course," Chuck said. "They'd have a dessert of some sort, and then he'd serve the coffee. Only he'd come in and he'd have the saucer in one hand and he'd be carrying the cup of coffee in the other, but he'd have his finger down in this steaming hot coffee. Anything for a gag, right?"

Neighbors also knew how zany Clellan could be. One Halloween around 1944, three ten-year-old friends of John Card's decided to stop at the Card house toward the end of the night. The light was still on, so they rang the doorbell. Clellan came to the door with a drink in his hand, looking very sophisticated in a gorgeous red velvet smoking jacket, complete with ascot. "Trick or treat!" the youngsters demanded. Clellan peered at the hobgoblins standing on his doorstep and said, "You know, I don't think there's anything left, but let me go back and check."

He went back into the house as the three kids whispered in excited anticipation, "This is gonna be great! If he doesn't have anything in there, he'll give us money!" which would be even better than candy. Before long Clellan returned, hiding something behind his back. He asked the kids to hold up their bags, which they did. Suddenly, in one smooth motion, he proceeded to pour champagne into all three bags. His hand went from one to the other and back again in an arc, "like it was a pendulum going back and forth and it was spilling champagne." It took just a moment for the paper bags to start collapsing. Clutching their bags tightly, the kids took off running for home. One of them, a youngster named Jim Lavin, ran through the back door of his house and banged all his stuff down on the kitchen table. His father heard the commotion and came into the room. As soon as he smelled the alcohol, he exclaimed, "What the hell have you been doing?"

The boy poured out the story of what had happened. Far from being upset about Clellan's Halloween trick, the elder Lavin thought the whole thing was hilarious. "I don't think I've ever seen my father laugh as hard. He threw his head back and just let out this guffaw,"

 What did you do when your wife stepped on the egg – beater?

Jim recalled. "That was the greatest Halloween I've ever had, and Clellan was the one that made it."

Radio director Bun Dawson was also treated to the Card hospitality. "In my early days at 'CCO, I worked a heavy schedule at both ends of the day, six days a week – for a big $25/week! – and so had little opportunity to meet people and make friends outside the station. Sensing this, Clell and Marion would sometimes invite me to spend Saturday night (my one free night) at their house on Colfax. They were that kind of people. In those days, the 'drinking hour' beverage was often a bottle of Sealect ('near beer') and an ounce or two of straight alcohol. You drank off a swig of Sealect, then poured the 'alky' in the bottle and tipped the bottle up. I remember tipping more than a few with the Cards over those years. Nobody ever got out of line, but in those days we were young and could handle it!"

In late 1939, Dawson had come from a trainee job at CBS-New York to work in Minneapolis at WCCO. One of his first assignments as a radio producer was on a show called *Curfew Time*, which had already premiered on September 25. It was a fifteen-minute show sponsored by Land O' Lakes, and it aired Monday through Friday at 10:15 P.M. *Curfew Time* was a small-scale musical variety program.

A publicity photo for *Curfew Time*. L to R: Toby Prin, the Plehal brothers, Don Allen, Irv Wickner, Eddie Gallaher, and Clellan.

What did you do when she kicked your foot – bawl?

the air at 7:00. After his morning chores he usually heads for home, breakfast, then to town again for a working day." That doesn't sound so hard, until you realize that in early 1940, his working day lasted until 10:30 P.M. when *Curfew Time* finished – a long stretch by anyone's standards. Even though Clellan probably had other opportunities to return home and relax during the course of the day, he was doing shows mornings, afternoons, and evenings, six days a week. He was also making frequent personal appearances at club luncheons, company dinners, and the like. It was a hectic schedule, but Clellan didn't complain. Odd hours were the price of being in the business. WCCO radio personality Bob DeHaven once remarked that radio announcers "don't do anything when other people do!"

In spite of everyone's hard work, Land O' Lakes was not happy with *Curfew Time*. Response from the public had been good; a telephone survey when the program was only four months old had shown that more than half of those listening to the radio at 10:15 P.M. were tuned to WCCO. Nevertheless, the weekly expense of the program was apparently more than the dairy giant had bargained for. Cost-cutting measures had been taken in early January 1940, but expenses were reduced by less than 10 percent. It wasn't enough, and Land O' Lakes eventually withdrew as the sponsor of the show. No suitable substitute could be found, so *Curfew Time* was off the air by July. Considering Clellan's workload, that was probably more a relief than a disappointment.

The cancellation had little effect on his career, which was on the verge of another milestone. Probably in late 1940 or early 1941,[10] Clellan began doing a comedy bit on *Almanac* that would become his lifelong trademark. Known as "the Birdie," it was adapted from a poem written by Robert Louis Stevenson:

TIME TO RISE

A birdie with a yellow bill
Hopped upon my windowsill,
Cocked his shining eye and said:
"Ain't you 'shamed, you sleepyhead!"

Marion had learned the quatrain in the second grade and often sang it to her children. Clellan appropriated the ditty for *Almanac of the Air*, but with a perverse twist. Each time he (or more often, his alter ego, Axel) recited it, the last line was changed to a different non

Clellan in the radio studio

sequitur pun, such as "Hey, I hear you took a bath – Matt!" or "What would you do if your wife drank – liquor?" Originally the gag was punctuated with the tweeting of a cuckoo birdcall, which later turned into Axel's spoken "Bee Boop!" finish.

Oddly enough, "the Birdie with a Yellow Bill" proved to be enormously popular. People actually enjoyed the atrocious puns – they were so bad, they were funny. Birdies became a fixture in Clellan's act, first on radio and later on the *Axel and His Dog* TV show. Over the years, he came up with hundreds of the wonderfully dreadful punch lines, although the claim that he conceived more than 12,000 of them and never used any of them more than once is a wild exaggeration. The silly rhyme became so closely identified with Clellan that, decades after his death, the mere mention of his name to Minnesotans born before 1960 often still prompts them to recite a Birdie.

While Clellan's career was going great guns, world events were taking a decidedly unfunny turn. When the United States entered World War II, Clellan (who had joined the U.S. Naval Reserve in the 1920s) wanted very much to join the Navy. Marion eventually dissuaded him, convincing him that a father with three young children was needed at home. But he did his part for the war effort in other ways, cheerfully donating his time to a variety of fund-raising and recruiting events.

He also recorded transcription disks that were shipped to far-flung military bases to give the dogfaces a taste of home. The Minnesota boys deeply appreciated these reminders of happier times. One soldier wrote about Clellan's efforts:

> We have not heard good old W.C.C.O. for more than 2 years. The world today needs laughs more than anything else, so you're really doing a good deed every morning whether you realize it or not.

  What did you do when you sat on the basket – bawl?

On February 10, 1943, another milestone was reached: the 2,000th *Almanac* broadcast. The Northrup, King program had been on the air for almost seven years. Clell had missed just fourteen shows in all that time, while a total of more than 40,320 "hardy" listeners had visited the studio at 7:00 A.M. to watch him do his stuff on the broadcasts.

Besides *Almanac*, Clellan continued to lend his talents to various other shows as well. In February 1944, a Saturday morning show called *Gab Session* and billed as "Clellan Card's good humor show," made its debut. He also took on the announcing chores on a music program called *Super-Mix Vocal-Aires*. The "Super-Mix" of the show's title, which gives the name a rather modern sound, actually referred to the sponsor, a brand of house paint. The Vocal-Aires, on the other hand, were the featured vocal group, singing the stylish arrangements of Ernie Garven in fluid harmonies. During the show, Clellan bantered with the singers – he particularly relished any opportunity to talk with the female members of the troupe – and delivered Super-Mix paint commercials in his familiar folksy manner. By now, talking on the radio was second nature to him. His future at WCCO seemed assured.

Then, suddenly, in the spring of 1944, *Almanac of the Air* was cancelled.

A publicity photo of Clellan at KSTP radio

CHAPTER 8

DUNKING AT THE
CARD TABLE

ALMANAC OF THE AIR cancelled! But why? Had Clellan's popularity started to slip? On Saturday, March 18, 1944, "only" about 700 souls, less than one-third the number of people who had shown up for the Doughnut Dunking Jamboree four years earlier, turned out for the "Special Doughnut Party Broadcast."

But that's not really a fair comparison. World War II was still raging, and it affected every aspect of life. While the first few jamborees had been strictly for fun, the 1944 party was primarily to promote WAVE enlistment and solicit contributions to the Red Cross. An article at the time termed the affair a "great success" and claimed that 700 "was a fine turnout considering that the temperature was only five above." Clell may not have been quite as popular as he once was, but he was still a favorite.

The real reason for the cancellation was that the Columbia Broadcasting System, WCCO's parent company, had pre-empted the 7:00 to 7:15 A.M. time slot for a world news program. Northrup, King was given the choice of sponsoring the news program or moving their *Almanac* program to some other period during the day. No other suitable time was available, so even though the new format was not as amenable to their commercials as the one they had enjoyed with Clellan, the company felt "compelled" to take the news show. In making the announcement, Northrup, King acknowledged that many people would be disappointed with the change of program but they implored, "we want everyone to know it was a situation forced upon us."

The final *Almanac of the Air* program was broadcast from the WCCO studios on Saturday, April 29. A sizable crowd turned out for the farewell dunkfest, but an air of melancholy lingered over the affair. All too soon, the show ended and Clellan Card's seven-and-a-half-year reign as the king of the early morning airwaves was over.

Meanwhile, a serious rival to WCCO had emerged: an up-and-coming station called KSTP. By 1944, its broadcasting power had grown to 50,000 watts, equalling WCCO's. The station had also recently established new radio studios in downtown Minneapolis, on the upper floors of the vacant Minnesota Theater, which had been renamed the Radio City Theater in deference to its new tenant. It was a suitable headquarters from which KSTP could begin a new assault on the seemingly impregnable ratings of its competitor.

Clellan continued to ply his trade on WCCO radio, but it just wasn't the same. *Almanac of the Air* had catapulted him to prominence, and the early morning time slot suited him. He yearned to return to his role as the mirth-meister of the morn, but WCCO hadn't offered him an adequate replacement for his defunct morning show. He began to consider the possibility of going freelance. As one of the top radio personalities in town, he knew that he would have little trouble finding work – it was no secret that KSTP had wanted him for some time.

In October of 1944, Clellan made the leap, becoming the first big-name freelancer in the Twin Cities in quite a while. He started at KSTP almost immediately, but apparently for a short time he also continued his commitments at WCCO. So Clell was heard on the area's two leading stations concurrently.

His stint at the new station began on October 16, as the announcer on *Clellan Card and the News*. It was broadcast Monday through Saturday from 12:30–12:45 p.m, directly opposite Cedric Adams, his former colleague (and ratings giant). Adams' wry humanity, eye for detail, and nasally intimate delivery had made him perhaps the best known and highest paid broadcaster on any single station in the United States. Unseating him was a tough assignment, but KSTP hoped that one of WCCO's own personalities could manage it. And Clellan's new employer was willing to pay him handsomely to make the attempt. One page of a 1945 FCC document reveals that, at $650

When you broke your leg, did you hop-a-long – Cassidy?

He couldn't get rid of the Birdie either, subjecting his KSTP audience to the same sort of excruciating puns that had built his career at WCCO. "What did you do with the Absorbine – Junior?" is a KSTP Birdie which (unfortunately?) has survived.

Jo Jones worked in KSTP's offices at the top of the St. Paul Hotel in those days, and got to know Clellan slightly. "He was a very handsome, immaculate man with a wonderful sense of humor," she remembered. "I think all the girls in the office were a little bit in love with him."

One particularly memorable incident involved Clellan and a young woman named Jeanette. "She was a lot of fun," Jo said. "All the guys would tease her, and she would tease 'em right back. And so, there was quite a camaraderie between her and the announcers. One morning, Clellan burst into the office – I think there were about six or seven of us girls in that one office – and he marched straight over to Jeanette, grabbed her, and leaned her backwards, and gave her a kiss that seemed to go on forever. And of course, the rest of us were just hooting and hollering and screaming. He put her back on her chair, turned and walked out of the office, and Jeanette – for once in her life – didn't have anything to say."

Ironically, the end of World War II was the beginning of the end for *Dunking at the Card Table*. During the war, an excess profits tax had been imposed on United States businesses to generate money for the war effort. If profits exceeded what was considered "normal" for a particular firm, the excess was taxed at an extremely high rate. Naturally, though, the costs of doing business were subtracted from gross reve-

Clellan, wearing a special microphone around his neck to keep his hands free, makes toast in the KSTP radio studio

 What are you carrying in all those bags, Morton – salt?

Clellan and Marion in the 1940s

nues before calculating the net profit. Employee wages were part of those costs, so if a business started generating higher earnings, hiring more people would lower profits and keep taxes down. At KSTP, rumor had it that employee ranks had swelled for just that reason. Since excess profits would be swallowed up by taxes anyway, it made sense for the station to mount elaborate productions in hopes that the extravaganzas would attract a larger audience.

When international hostilities ceased, however, the excess profits tax was repealed and any incentive to maintain bloated employee rolls vanished with it. *Dunking at the Card Table*, with its large and expensive contingent of musicians, soon felt the ax. At the close of 1945, everyone was laid off except Clellan, second banana Jimmy Valentine, and bandleader Leonard Leigh. The show's length also was slashed from an hour to a mere fifteen minutes.

However, KSTP gave Clellan another show immediately, one that took advantage of his forte of talking to people, called *Clellan Card's Morning Gab Fest*. Instead of broadcasting from a radio studio, it took place on the street. The format of the forty-five-minute presentation was similar to that of the earlier WCCO program *Meet the Missus*. Clell would interview people about themselves, events around town, or whatever else came to mind. Jimmy Valentine tagged along with him. "I was the bird dog," he recalled. "I would accost people, 'cause that's the big job on that sort of show, getting somebody to stop. You push a mike in their face and they fall over the curb getting away from you, you know. So I would go out and smile and say, 'It's Clellan Card! C'mon over and talk to him.'"

Morning Gab Fest was a good vehicle for Clellan, but things had taken a turn for the worse for him at KSTP. Not only had *Dunking at the Card Table* been drastically reduced, he was being clobbered by Cedric Adams in the noon news competition. In July 1946, KSTP finally conceded defeat in the noontime battle, canceling *Clellan Card and the News*. Not long after that, another series of cost-cutting measures were imposed at the station – supposedly because station founder Stanley Hubbard needed cash to acquire the 75 percent of KSTP stock that he didn't own. Two engineers, two announcers, six pages and receptionists, one newsroom employee, and one person in the promotion department were let go. The station's hours of operation were trimmed, and its promotion sheet, *Radio Reporter*, was dropped. Almost as an afterthought, the remnant of *Dunking at the Card Table* was killed.[11]

Clellan soldiered on with *Morning Gab Fest*, but his future at KSTP seemed increasingly tenuous. Meanwhile, WCCO radio had been stung by a string of high-profile resignations, nearly climaxed by the defection of top broadcaster Cedric Adams to – of all places – KSTP. After narrowly averting that disaster by acceding to all of the folksy commentator's demands, WCCO wanted to shore up its position as the undisputed Twin Cities radio ratings champ. The exodus of personnel from the station had begun with Clellan's departure, so they may have reasoned that rehiring him would help reverse the trend. Even though he hadn't been wildly successful at KSTP, he was still one of the Twin Cities' best-known personalities. So, in August 1947, it was announced that Clellan Card would return to WCCO radio the following month.

Clellan and Arthur Godfrey in 1949, cribbing jokes from *Cracks by Card*

CHAPTER 9

FROM SPINNER SANCTUM TO THE BOOB TUBE

CLELLAN RETURNED TO WCCO a little ahead of schedule. To commemorate his return to the fold with as much fanfare as possible, a special radio broadcast from the Minnesota State Fair kicked things off at the end of August. As a preview of his forthcoming *Man on the Street* program, he wandered the fairgrounds interviewing people.

At 11:30 P.M. on Monday, September 1, 1947, Clellan officially debuted on WCCO radio as a late-night disc jockey on the *Clellan Card Midnite Show*. The new program was the successor to the *Night Owls Show*, which had had a "club" membership of over 100,000 listeners in every state of the Union. A newspaper ad heralded his return with overheated hyperbole: "What a man! He's riding the discs now, and YOU are going to LOVE it." Monday through Saturday, Clell played hot tunes and cool jazz until one o'clock in the morning, introducing the songs in a mellow tone well suited to the wee hours. He often conducted interviews with band leaders or celebrities of stage and screen, enlivening things with his spontaneous ad libs. One fan of the show was an aspiring young singer named Mary Davies. "I just loved his voice and always thought he was so great," she remembered.

Clellan's interest in music was genuine, nurtured by his musically inclined father. His enthusiasm was abetted by the record companies, which were happy to send him promotional copies of their latest releases in the hopes that he would deign to play them on one of his radio programs. By the late 1940s, the sunroom of the Card house

What would you do if your teacher got in your airplane – hangar?

on Colfax Avenue was a spectacular library of about 3,000 78-rpm records, from Cole Porter standards to the latest jazz, all carefully filed. In contrast to the casual atmosphere that prevailed in the rest of the house, young visitors were warned not to violate the sanctity of Clellan's private den.

Once, Clellan's son Michael and a few of his friends tempted fate by attempting to use his father's Capehart record player. It was an elaborate device that could lift a disc off the turntable, flip it over, replace the record on the spindle, and play the other side. Unluckily, the mechanism went out of control and shattered some of the fragile records. The panicked kids turned off the machine before it could do any more damage and prayed that Clellan wouldn't find out what they had done.

As a publicity gimmick to spark interest in Clellan's *Midnite Show*, WCCO announced a contest to rename the program, with a $200 state-of-the-art RCA Victor radio-phonograph offered as first prize. The winner was an insurance agent from Lake City. After appearing on the show to collect his prize, the agent returned to his home town on the shores of Lake Pepin where he was "greeted by a band, hoisted into a convertible, and conducted on a 15-car parade through the city." The winning entry was truly inspired: a cunning pun on a then-popular horror radio program called *Inner Sanctum* that alluded to playing phonograph records. Henceforth, Clell's show would be known as *Spinner Sanctum*.

Even though he was burning the midnight oil on *Spinner Sanctum* six nights a week, it wasn't long before Clell was back on the early morning shift as well. He was recruited as the host of *The Marshall-Wells Show*, another dawn variety program. Every Tuesday, Thursday, and Saturday morning at 6:45 A.M., Clellan supplied the humor while Bob Link, Burt Hanson, Dick Link, and Eddie Fortier provided the music. It was probably on *The Marshall-Wells Show* that another familiar voice made a welcome return to the Minnesota airwaves. Not heard from during the KSTP years, Axel barged back onto the radio as the resident idiot savant of the program, where he regularly delivered Birdies.

Clellan began hosting his new WCCO radio program called *Man on the Street* as well, broadcast Monday through Friday at 5:15 P.M. The show was similar to *Clellan Card's Morning Gab Fest*, which itself

The Marshall-Wells gang: Clellan, singers Bob Link, Burt Hanson, and Dick Link, and pianist Eddie Fortier

had resembled the earlier *Meet the Missus.* By any name, it was Clellan doing what he did best. "Have a chat with the man with the fast come-back!" coaxed one ad.

As the name indicates, *Man on the Street* took place on the street, most often in front of the Century Theater. During the fifteen-minute presentation, Clellan usually found himself talking to young women – hardly an onerous task for him. Michael Card recalled, "There were two types of girls that would be interviewed on the show: one was the girl who was in from the farm to do some shopping, and they're

What are you digging, Marshall ~ Wells?

Bob DeHaven and Clellan duke it out on *Quiz of the Twin Cities*

the greatest people to talk to; and the other was the secretary that worked in the office buildings around there. As Dad's show gained popularity, these girls would show up in huge numbers, long before showtime, and Dad would pull up with all the equipment and his engineer and all that kind of stuff and have to fight his way through the crowd to get set up for this show. His sponsor was Butternut Coffee ("the coffee delicious"), and he would give away pound tins of Butternut Coffee to his guests as prizes for being on the show."

By October 1947, Clellan also became the co-host of *Quiz of the Twin Cities*, a Tuesday night game show that pitted perennial rivals Minneapolis and St. Paul against each other. Despite being a lifelong Minneapolitan, Clell led the St. Paul crew while jovial Bob DeHaven was captain of the Minneapolis players. The opponents battled over the airwaves – literally. The Minneapolis team vied for prizes from WCCO radio's fourth-floor auditorium, while the St. Paul team competed across the Mississippi River in the studios located in the Hotel Lowry.

To a listener, the career of a radio personality might have sounded like the life of Riley: the star simply showed up at the appointed

Saturday evening radio program broadcast from the American House in St. Paul. Typically, a paying crowd of perhaps three or four hundred people, mostly of German or Polish extraction, came to dance. The band would start playing at about 8:00 P.M., get the crowd warmed up for an hour or so, and then do the broadcast. On at least one occasion, the irrepressible Card allegedly couldn't resist cracking a joke about the bandleader's Germanic surname. Broadcaster Rodger

Whoopee John Wilfahrt watching Cedric Adams drive the bus

Kent claimed that he nearly drove off the road when he heard Clellan introduce the show by saying, "And now, Whoopee John Wilfahrt – and his band will play!"

Not surprisingly, at WTCN Clell was the host of a morning radio program, this time called simply *The Clellan Card Show*. As usual, he would play a few records, chitchat, and tell some jokes. The carefree Card's habit of arriving just before airtime proved a bit nerve-wracking for audio engineer John Sieberz. "Clellan was always late, and I'd almost have a heart attack working that show, 'cause I never knew whether he was gonna make it or not. He had a habit of waiting until the last second before he went on the air. I didn't have the records, I didn't know whether Clellan was even in the building or not. All of a sudden he'd run up the stairs and give me a couple of records, and he'd run downstairs, and I'd play his theme and open the mike, and he'd do the show." Sieberz laughed, "I was really sweating by about that time!"

As Clellan had hoped, WTCN also gave him the opportunity to begin working in television. His first regular TV series aired Wednesday afternoons, beginning about May 24, 1950. The program was called *Stop, Look and Listen*, although it was also known as (surprise!) *The Clellan Card Show.*

This was television's Stone Age. The title cards for *Stop, Look and Listen* were crudely hand-lettered placards, which Clellan would flip one by one during the opening of the show. However, his sense of humor survived the switch to TV intact. One reviewer wrote, "Clellan Card is one of the quietest atom bombs I have

Clellan talking to one of his guests on *Stop, Look and Listen*

encountered. The opening monologue on his Wednesday 4:30 P.M. show is sprinkled generously with lazily emitted explosive remarks which are quite priceless!"

The show had no studio audience, so to generate some on-air laughter Clell had to try to break up the crew. He often succeeded, although on at least one occasion they punctuated a gag by dumping tin cans into a wastebasket. On the other hand, they kept themselves amused by trying to rattle him while he was on-camera. One day, a stagehand ostentatiously ate a lemon while Clellan was on the air, in a good-natured effort to sour the host's speech. During another broadcast, one crewman even took his pants off – but failed to make Clellan lose his cool.

Encompassing "interesting interviews, jokes, and demonstrations of adorable toys, and anything else he decides upon on the spur of the moment," the TV show bore more than a passing resemblance to Clellan's radio gigs, and had an air of casual wackiness that took advantage of TV's visual possibilities. On one installment, he wore a rubber lizard on his lapel for no apparent reason. On another, he had a member of the Minneapolis police motorcycle squad ride his cycle into WTCN-TV's studio as a preface to an interview about school and traffic safety. The program also featured "storybook tales for tots," marking Clellan's first tentative venture into children's television.

He also adapted his tried-and-true *Man on the Street* radio interview formula to television on a show called *Sidewalk Interviews* (or – you guessed it – *The Clellan Card Show*). This Channel 4 program had the distinction of being the first and only outdoor interview TV show in the upper Midwest. Considering that it was conducted outside even in sub-zero weather, perhaps its singular status isn't too surprising.

Newscaster Dave Moore remembered well what TV was like in those early days. "There was no videotape, and there were no teleprompters, so from a performer's standpoint, you had to do it right there. If you walked into the lobby of our studios on Ninth and LaSalle of an early evening, it would not be unusual to see two or three people walking back and forth mumbling, as though they were institutionalized someplace, talking to themselves. What they were doing was learning commercials: mumbling to themselves, getting the commercials. Then they'd get the call, go in the studio,

What did you do when you ate the cream – puff?

Dave Moore

take a quick run-through in the rehearsal – a run-through of the commercial on-camera – and then when there was a break in the movie, you'd do the commercial. If you blow it, you blow it – but you can't do it again."

Dave credited his background in theater with preparing him for the rigors of working in live television. "My discipline insisted that I learn lines, learn copy, learn the material, and I developed a technique for becoming a rather quick study. All of us were: Mel Jass, Bud Kraehling, John Gallos, Clellan, myself. All of us who performed on-camera had to have this facility for learning lines, and keeping our cool, and doing it."

While his new career on television was beginning, Clellan also enjoyed some good times with his father. On October 26, 1949, the Apollo Club honored the esteemed Dr. Card with a dinner at the Interlachen Club in recognition of his fifty years of singing with the organization. The following week, Clellan was the master of ceremonies at the seventy-fifth anniversary celebration of Adams school (the oldest in Minneapolis then still in use) featuring former pupil Dr. William Card as one of the guests.

Even in his sixties, Bill Card was always ready for family fun. Spending the winter months in the Curtis Hotel by then, he and Ina summered in their cottage on the shores of Lake Minnetonka, where they delighted in frequent visits from Clellan's clan. Daddy Bill was also happy to trudge into the woods with his grandsons for target practice, demonstrating the finer points of handling a firearm. The aged but avid golfer often spent time on the links with Clellan, who shared his dad's love of the game.

Portly, mustachioed Dr. Card was known for his wry humor and sharp wit – it was said that his son "got his guff" from his old man. He had remained active as a dentist for fifty-two years, becoming one

What color is snow – white?

"Daddy Bill" and Ina Card

of the oldest practicing in Minnesota. Declining health finally forced him to retire to his lakeside home in Meadville, where he died on June 1, 1950, after a brief illness. Since he was by then seventy-one years old, Daddy Bill's passing was not entirely unexpected, but it was a blow all the same. All his life, Clellan had had an unusually close relationship with his father. His dad's death probably seemed like the worst thing that had ever happened.

Michael, Peter, and John Card

CHAPTER 10

The END oF THE GOOD OLD DAYS

CLELLAN CARD LOVED HIS FAMILY more than anything in the world. A 1945 magazine article claimed that "Clellan has no hobbies, except his home and family. One of the ways he likes to spend the time he's not on the air or preparing for his programs is reading the comics to his children." The photo accompanying the article shows just that: the old man lying on the floor reading comic books with his kids – all of them wearing suits!

Clellan joked that he had "three sons and one wife," but it was clear that he and Marion loved each other dearly. "If my parents had problems, we never knew about it," Michael Card declared, "and if we had problems, we could always share 'em with the folks and then they wouldn't be problems anymore. It was the kind of upbringing that I think most people wish they could have."

The Card house was a home very much in the Ozzie and Harriet mold. Friends remember it as a warm and welcoming place, the center of fun in the neighborhood. It was a house where milk and cookies always seemed to be on the kitchen table, and a wrestling match in the living room wasn't frowned upon (well, not much, anyway). The Cards had the first television set on the block and they were happy to share it. They even had a slot machine on the basement bar. Clellan set the tone, constantly clowning to everyone's delight. Michael's childhood pal Noel Allard said, "I learned from him that laughter is more precious than anything."

The three Card kids were a happily mixed bag. Clellan Peter, the

Marion, Michael, Clellan, Peter, and John Card in 1945

oldest (always known by his middle name) was the serious, intellectual one. "He was really into books," Michael said of his eldest brother, "he was into philosophies, he was into classics. He just devoured literature." Jerry Walsh, a high school friend, declared simply, "He was a young gentleman. He had class." Pete's hooded eyes and sharp-featured face, topped by closely cropped brown hair, gave him a slightly sinister appearance that belied his good-natured disposition.

But Peter knew how to have fun. His buddy Stanley Tull described how they used to make swords and shields out of old crate boxes: "We'd run down to 50th and Bryant to the grocery store and go through their bin in the back and bring home orange crates and knock the quarter-inch boards off of the side. The one-inch boards on the ends, we'd take the bands off, the steel bands, and nail 'em on the back so we could hang onto 'em." Then the backyard battles would begin!

Clellan would play with the kids whenever he could. "Mr. Card would come down every once in a while – he was a pretty busy guy.

When did you first fall in love with the old bean – bag?

"It was more important to him to have fun, and that's what he did: he got average grades and had a heck of a lot of fun and was extremely popular." His senior yearbook called him the class wit, but his glib quips masked a sensitive young man. At least one of his friends believes that John felt the social pressures and slights of adolescence more acutely than most. "John was a good guy, I liked him – I mean, you know, everybody did – but he was kind of a moody guy," Chuck declared. "He could get a little morose from one time to the next. I think a lot of these guys that we ran with just kind of bulldozed ahead, and John didn't. He was possibly more introspective somehow."

Pete went on to college on September 29, 1947, enrolling at the University of Minnesota. Unfortunately, his college career seemed to be patterned more after his father's than his grandfather's. He had done well in high school, winning a number of essay contests, but college was a struggle. As a freshman, the highest grade he got was a C. In the spring quarter of 1948 he cancelled three out of four classes, and failed the last. The result was academic probation. After another lackluster quarter in the fall of 1948, Pete was "dropped for low scholarship." In the spring of 1949, he re-enrolled. For a while he acquitted himself well, earning his first A, in a writing course. Within a year, however, things had deteriorated to the point that he was placed on "strict" probation. Summer sessions did nothing to help the situation; by this time, Pete seemed to have lost interest in college. He flunked out after the fall quarter of 1950.

Like many people his age, Pete seemed to find the real world more appealing than school and there was one particular corner of the globe that he found especially fascinating: England. He had been an Anglophile for as long as anyone could remember. "When I get to England ..." became his mantra. He even studied Gaelic, the native tongue of the ancient Celts. Finally, in 1951, he realized his life's dream. "Pete and I went to New York just before he went into the service," recalled his friend Jerry Walsh. "He wanted to go to England on the Queen Mary, so I went to see him off." Peter did the usual tourist stuff in London, and travelled all over the countryside.

After he returned from England, he enlisted in the U.S. Air Force. "Peter was in love with flying long before he ever flew, and he always had envisioned himself as being a pilot," Michael said, "so he decided

Why don't you use your bean – pot?

he was going to be in the Air Force." Peter went down to Texas for basic training, and eventually was assigned to Goodfellow Air Force base outside of San Angelo, Texas. He began flying T-6s, tandem two-seat propeller fighter planes, which were "highly aerobatic, not very fast, and very squirrelly at low speeds – you really learn your skills in a T-6."

By early September, 1952, Pete had nearly completed the first phase of his training and had just gotten his wings. Michael remembered that Pete "was about a week away from being transferred into jet school and he was so excited he couldn't stand it." He was to be commissioned as an Air Force pilot in December.

The young flyer was proud of his accomplishment, and with good reason. Of the nineteen cadets in his class, only four would graduate.

Cadet Peter Card

Four others quit, five apparently washed out – and, ultimately, six were killed. Some felt that the high attrition rate was at least partly due to insufficient training. "In the Korean War, they were pushing them so hard to get them through and out, they just really didn't train them adequately," contended Clellan's cousin, Bill Card.

On the morning of September 9, 1952, Peter had taken off at 7:30 A.M. for a two-hour solo flight, trying to get in as much flying time as possible before his transfer to jet school. He had just returned to the base when fellow cadet and friend Robert Beaubien, who also had recently earned his wings, asked Pete to fly with him as a check pilot in a T-6 aircraft. The check pilot sits in the tandem cockpit behind the pilot, watching for other aircraft and cloud clearance, so the pilot can practice flying using only his instruments, with his head under a hood to prevent him from seeing outside the aircraft. Pete loved to fly, so he jumped at the opportunity to go up again.

After about an hour of flight, Bob Beaubien had finished his instrument training, taken his hood off, and was once again in command of the plane under visual flight rules. Pete, his check pilot duties completed, had essentially become a passenger in the aircraft. At about 11:15 A.M., they were coming in for a landing when something went terribly wrong. According to witnesses, the plane approached the field at approximately 800 feet, preparing for a landing, and then banked in to final approach. The mobile command officer noted that the turn was made in an unusually nose-high attitude. The aircraft snapped to the right and then effected a partial recovery in a nose-low attitude. Suddenly one of the wings stalled, sending the aircraft into a spin. Like Peter, Beaubien was an above-average student who had approximately 185 hours of flying time, and he could have recovered easily from that sort of mishap at five thousand feet. At less than 1,000 feet up, however, there simply wasn't time. The plane spun into the ground, and exploded and burned on impact. Both of the young men perished. Peter Card was just twenty-three.

That evening, the Card family was sitting down to dinner when one of their neighbors knocked at the door. The fateful telegram had been delivered to his house by mistake; he had unwittingly opened it and read the terrible news about Peter. Ashen-faced, he could only hand the message to Clellan and stammer, "This is for you."

Somehow, funeral arrangements were made. Friends were publicly invited to call at the Card residence the night before the funeral for the recitation of the Rosary. Unfortunately, the experience proved to be an encounter with the darker side of local celebrity. Because of Clellan's very public career, news of the tragedy was well known. Michael recalled with some bitterness, "Strangers walked in and looked around and walked back out. It was bizarre. People have lots of curiosity and no sensitivity at all."

Peter's funeral was held on Saturday, September 13th. It was a warm late-summer day; by the time that services began in the Church of the Visitation at ten o'clock that morning, the temperature had already soared to more than 80 degrees. Following the service, interment took place at Resurrection Cemetery in Mendota Heights, quite far from the church. Peter's grave was about halfway up a gently sloping hillside, near the shade of an arching elm tree. The mourners gathered at the gravesite, and as the pallbearers held the flag which had draped the coffin, some distance away a bugler played taps. Pallbearer Jim Lavin recalled, "Our knees just gave out. It was one of the saddest moments. And I remember Marion – she just about collapsed when they played that."

Chuck Stanek, another pallbearer, also remembered how distraught Peter's mother was. "God, I never felt so bad for anybody in my life as for Marion," he said. "I thought, I really thought, this woman was in so much pain, I thought she was going to die any time herself. She was just disconsolate over Peter's death."

Jerry Walsh, remembering his friend Peter, said in a voice choked with emotion, "He stays forever young in your mind, that's what's kind of strange. He didn't grow old with the rest of us."

The Card household, the scene of so much fun and laughter, was suddenly transformed into a desolate landscape of grief. Michael set up a makeshift shrine to his oldest sibling in his bedroom. The normally ebullient John, shattered by the loss of his big brother, became withdrawn. And like his wife, Clellan was hard hit. For once, humor failed him as he tried to come to grips with the awful tragedy of losing a child.

After a few months, life slowly began to return to normal. Michael vividly remembered what happened next: "My parents, in order to promote their own healing, decided after Christmas [1952] to go out to the West Coast and visit some friends. My brother John, who was just devastated by Peter's death – I mean, it really hit him hard, and he's a very up guy, very up; it was really hard to get John down – was struggling very much. I was only thirteen and I really wasn't capable of feeling the kinds of things that John felt at the age of eighteen. So, we decided to go to California on the train. It was a great trip – I got very close to my brother John. He taught me how to shave. I had these white little peach-fuzzy whiskers. John led me through all the manly steps of using the Gillette double-edged razor: how to put on the shave cream and soften the beard, and all that kind of stuff. Kind of a special time."

On the first part of the trip, they visited a childhood friend of Marion's in Arcadia, California. After that, Clellan, Marion, and Michael went on to the Desert Willow Guest Ranch in Tucson, Arizona, a place where they had vacationed before. John, however, had to fly back to Minneapolis to begin a new semester at St. Thomas College, where he was studying engineering.

CHAPTER 11

BiRDiE, THy NAMe Is TORGESON

THE NEXT FEW MONTHS were, without a doubt, the most difficult of Clellan's life. The jocular joker was plunged into black despair. No gag was funny enough to penetrate the gloom, and Marion was incapable of doing much to help. She had done her best after Peter's death, but when John was killed, too, she fell apart. Grief-stricken himself, Clell had to console her as best he could. Their love for each other helped them endure, and as they struggled to come to terms with their loss, their Catholic faith also gave them solace and strength – but nothing could bring back their sons. The life they had known was gone forever.

"I think my parents were so devastated by what had happened to them that they kind of lost their will to fight," reflected Michael. "And I perceive that time in my life, between the ages of thirteen and eighteen – which is a long, long time for a kid – as a time when my parents were too liberal with me. They were not strict enough. And I think the reason for that is that they just thought, 'Que sera. It's totally out of our hands anyway – if he goes out and kills himself, okay. That's three out of three.' For thirteen years, the rules were the rules and I understood them very, very clearly. But after Peter and John died, the rules weren't the rules. There *weren't* any rules."

Clellan seemed almost visibly deflated. Friends and neighbors noticed the change in him. Chuck Stanek declared, "I don't think Clellan was ever quite the same after that." Jim Lavin agreed, saying, "There was just a sadness to him." As if things weren't bad enough, some very unpleasant letters arrived in the mail. A few unthinking people accused Clellan of somehow being responsible for John's accident because he had been doing beer commercials on the radio.

It was all too much. Clellan became so despondent that he even contemplated suicide. Such an act was completely contrary to his nature, not to mention the strictures of the Catholic Church, but life had stopped making sense to him. One day, feeling especially hopeless, he seriously suggested to Marion, "Let's just walk into the lake and drown." Fortunately, she managed to dissuade him.

Shortly before the Card family's nightmare began, Clellan's professional situation had undergone upheaval as well. In August 1952, Midwest Radio-Television Inc. (the owner of WTCN-TV and WTCN radio) purchased a 53-percent interest in WCCO radio from CBS. Midwest Radio-Television then divested itself of WTCN radio and changed the call letters of its television station to WCCO to match its newly acquired radio station, which was still a ratings titan. Clellan stayed with the television station, so when WTCN-TV became WCCO-TV on August 17, he found himself back at WCCO by default. Peter's plane crash came less than a month later.

In the depths of his depression, Clellan went to see F. Van Konynenburg, the executive vice president at WCCO-TV, and announced that he could not go on the air anymore. He intended to quit the business. As friend and co-worker Don Stolz told the story, Van Konynenburg responded by saying, "Clellan, I understand that you're grieving, but you are going *on.* I have a contract with you and if you quit, I'll sue you for every penny you've got. In fact, I've already given you a month off – you're starting next week."

"He had no intention of suing Clellan, of course," Don hastened to add. "What he wanted to do was to get Clellan back in *life* again. And it worked." At first Clell was taken aback by Van Konynenburg's seemingly hardhearted attitude, but he did return to work. Eventually, after thinking things over, he thanked "Mr. Van" for forcing him to go back on the air. He later told Don that it was "the kindest thing that could have happened."

Besides appearing on the newly renamed WCCO-TV, Clellan returned to WCCO radio in February 1953. He began as the host of two new shows: *Pop the Question* and *Card's Corral. Pop the Question* was a five-minute evening program that brought on a guest expert to vide comedy relief. A running gag was soon established: Olaf would shuffle across the set at random, silently pushing a broom, staring at the floor, and invariably prompting Mel to yell, "Somebody get Olaf out of here! We're trying to do a show!"

Television may have been a new medium, but Clellan still relied on the same kind of jokes that he'd used on radio for more than twenty years. One April Fools' Day, Olaf elaborately complained to "Mr. Yass" about how "wore out" he was. Mel – the proper straight man – asked, "What's the trouble? What's the matter with you?" The janitor retorted, "Well, who wouldn't be tired after a March of tirty-one days!"

Clellan had been doing female voices on the radio since the *Almanac* days and now on television, he regaled viewers with characters such as Cecilia "Grandma" Sykes, a bilious old crone with a fondness for playing pool. Parked in a rocking chair, swathed in a crocheted shawl, a small flowered bonnet roosting atop her gray locks, Grandma spun convoluted yarns in a quavery voice punctuated with a whistling lisp caused by her ill-fitting dentures.

He developed a female character for *The Mel Jass Show* who was known by the unlikely name of Jessica Jigglebustle. "She" was an obnoxious gossip with a voice that had all the charm of a mosquito in a tent at midnight. The old biddy wore a frowzy, frumpy dress, her long white hair done up in large ringlets and covered with a kerchief. Toby played Jessica's neighbor, Prunella, dressed in a gingham checked dress with a matching sunbonnet. The two shrews would meet in the back yard while hanging their wash. During these encounters, Jessica did most of the talking, which was considerable, while Prunella offered only an occasional monosyllable.

For a time in the mid-1950s, Mel's half-hour show was followed by one hosted by the young broadcaster Dave Moore. *The Dave Moore Show* differed from *The Mel Jass Show* mainly in the eponymous host; otherwise, the two programs were quite similar, using many of the same personnel. Olaf the Janitor blundered onto Dave's set just the way he did Mel's, and told "bad jokes, really. Cardinally stale jokes," Dave admitted. "But because they were told, they were funny and they got a laugh from everyone."

Dave remembered his variety show as "a really freewheeling, totally spontaneous program – far more than it should have been.

 Have you finished with your shaving – mug?

Toby Prin as Prunella and Clellan as Jessica Jigglebustle

Little as I tried to plan, and produce, and lay out sketches and ideas, you know, television eats these things up so quickly and spits them out. But the program was important, as we view it retrospectively, because it was locally produced. It was like, 'C'mon, gang! Hey, let's put on a show!' You know, the Judy Garland–Mickey Rooney kind of thing. It had that flavor to it."

A young father in those days, Dave occasionally would bring one of his children to the set. Once, while doing the show, he glanced off-camera to see Clellan changing his child's diaper. Nothing seemed to faze the old pro. "He was a very casual, cool person," noted Dave. "It wasn't a studied calmness; he was just very loose. He had a gag for everything." Like others who knew Clellan, Dave Moore also discovered that there was more lurking beneath the silly getups than most people would guess. "He was quite a bright fellow. Off-mike, many of his lines and ideas of humor were based on something as obscure as Greek mythology or the Prussian military. He had a wonderful sense of history."

Clellan created still another character who appeared on various WCCO-TV programs: a daffy, dimwitted football coach named Teakwood Torgeson. Attired in a ratty raccoon coat, a bristly mustache on his lip, and a too-small football helmet or oversize baseball cap askew on his head, Teakwood cut a ridiculous figure. The coach's appearance was not his only idiotic aspect. Teakwood's routines proved that vaudeville wasn't dead; it had simply moved to television. A case in point survives in an installment of the sports program *Roundy Predicts*, broadcast one Thanksgiving Day.

After a brief introduction by announcer Randy Merriman, who promised viewers "something very special, one of the greatest coaches in the entire United States," the bulldog-like visage of renowned Minnesota sportscaster Halsey Hall appeared, standing in a dingy locker room. Halsey invested the moment with the requisite gravity as he announced in his gravelly wheeze, "And here he is, ladies and gentlemen, the idol of football fans the country over, the outstanding mentor of Destitute Institute, Teakwood Torgeson."

Teakwood strode in, tooting a whistle strung around his neck. His incongruous baseball cap sat cockeyed atop his head, and his mustache seemed to be crooked as well. His raccoon coat was unbuttoned, revealing a potbelly underneath his tight sweatshirt. As the two men shook hands, Teakwood chuckled moronically. Then, acknowledging the applause from the small audience, the coach did a little dance. Abruptly, he turned to Halsey and demanded, "How are you, Hall, you old bum?"

Ignoring the question, Halsey plunged into the interview. "Now, first of all, Coach, I wanna congratulate you on your undefeated season at Destitute Institute."

Teakwood swelled with pride as he confirmed, "Yah, we was, uh, we was – we ain't defeated nobody for nine years."

"You've had a great career, Coach Torgeson," Halsey remarked, sounding a bit dubious. "What outstanding thing can you recall, as a player, would you name as your greatest thrill?"

Teakwood seemed momentarily confused by the question, but regained his composure. "Well, it was when I was playin' at old P.U.,

 What's for dinner, Mother – goose?

Teakwood Torgeson being interviewed by Halsey Hall

it was. That time I was playin' there, and one of our biggest games, it was, we was playin' a school called Hardly Normal, it was.

"And the coach told me to get into the game," he said, pounding his fist for emphasis. "He says to me, he says, 'Teakwood, get into the game! It might save the day!' See, that's what he says to me, see?

"And I'm sittin' right there on the bench, see, and I'm all full of ambition and fight and everyting. So the crowd cheered and roared and everyting and I'm rushin' out on the field for old P.U. And I rushed right out on the field and everything there, see like that, and the crowd roared."

"And that was your greatest thrill?" wondered Halsey. "Because it was your last game, I suppose."

"No," Teakwood said, "because I forgot my pants that time!"

Halsey looked askance at the coach. "Well," he noted caustically, "with your head, they were sure of one point, anyway."

The oafish Teakwood was one of a long line of Torgesons[13] roaming the ether. The dizzy dynasty may date as far back as the 1930s, when Peggy Beckmark created a situation comedy for WCCO radio called *Tena and Tim* about the tribulations of a wealthy dowager and her bumbling Swedish maid and Irish handyman. The show became so popular that it went into syndication, and in August 1944 CBS picked it up for a two-year hitch on the network. Creator Beckmark played the maid, who was named Tena Torgeson.

Clellan was certainly familiar with the *Tena and Tim* show; in fact, he stole at least one gag from it.[14] It's possible that he chose the Torgeson name as a backhanded tribute to Peggy Benchmark's show. It might have amused him to imagine that his own characters were the illegitimate children of WCCO's silly Swedish servant. However, at this late date, there's no way to be certain that Tena was the ancestor of Clellan's Torgesons. If she wasn't, though, the identical surnames are quite a coincidence.

What did you do with that car – bumper?

Once Clellan had appropriated the Torgeson name, the tribe grew faster than mold on a spoiled orange. Coach Teakwood and Olaf the Janitor of *The Mel Jass Show* were both Torgesons, clearly spawned from the same polluted gene pool. A "Doctor" Torgeson occasionally delivered loopy lectures on Mel's show, although he bore a suspicious resemblance to Olaf wearing a top hat and tails over his overalls. Leopold Torgeson, "the world's newest conductor," made a one-shot appearance

Doctor Torgeson

at a Minneapolis Symphony Orchestra luncheon. He looked a bit like Albert Einstein on a bad hair day, but was really a parody of the famous conductor Leopold Stokowski. Feisty Grandma Torgeson, the keeper of all the arcane and absurd Torgeson family lore, made regular appearances on *Axel and His Dog* and she supposedly originated the Scandihoovian version of "Twas the Night Before Christmas." There seemed to be no end of Torgesons. If the "Birdie with a yellow bill" had a surname, it must have been Torgeson.

One member of the clan, however, tottered above all the rest: Axel.

Don Stolz and Clellan during the premiere episode of *Axel and His Dog*

THE BiRTh oF AxEL aND HiS DoG

THE GOLDEN AGE OF TELEVISION coincided with the baby boom. The NBC program *Howdy Doody* had premiered on December 27, 1947, and in the wake of that freckle-faced marionette's incredible success, children's shows began popping up all over the dial. In addition to countless network programs, local shows also kept young baby boomers across the country glued to their TV sets. Most local television stations produced at least one kiddie show in the early years of television, to fill air time if nothing else. Typically, such programs were hosted by an adult dressed in a funny costume who horsed around, introduced film shorts or cartoons, and (most importantly) did commercials. Sponsors were quick to realize how effectively kiddie characters promoted products. Thanks to the sheer number of baby boomers watching TV, children's programs supplied stations with ratings, revenue, and even prestige. Kids' shows had a certain cachet in those days.

In the Twin Cities, the first children's television show aired on KSTP-TV, Channel 5, on May 8, 1948. *Riddle Griddle* was a quiz show for kids that had originated on radio, emceed in both mediums by Clellan's erstwhile announcer Jimmy Valentine, who was "the Riddle Master." *Jimmy's Junior Jamboree*, another Channel 5 offering, followed in September 1949, and was also hosted by Valentine.

For its part, Channel 4 (at the time, still WTCN-TV) put amiable Toby Prin on the kidvid beat. One of his earliest television shows aimed at children was called *Mailbox Melodies*, which premiered on

 What did you do with the light – socket?

Jimmy Valentine (left) and friends on
Jimmy's Junior Jamboree in late 1950

August 22, 1949. Its sole gimmick seems scarcely believable today. The audience sent in song requests, along with a photo. The picture would be displayed while Toby sang and played the tune. That's it – that was the whole show. Still, the young viewers of the era apparently loved it. In its first eight months on the air, the show received more than 5,000 pictures.

The original WTCN-TV (Channel 4) was transformed into WCCO-TV in August 1952, but on September 1, 1953, a reborn WTCN-TV re-entered the fray as Channel 11. The new station wasted little time in joining the race for kiddie viewers. Before the year was out, Daryl Laub created *Skipper Daryl*, allegedly the first kids' show in the Twin Cities to feature a costumed character, for Channel 11. Soon he added a tattered clown called J. P. Patches to the roster as well.

On May 14, 1954, one of the Twin Cities' best-remembered children's characters appeared on WTCN-TV for the first time: engineer Casey Jones, played by Roger Awsumb. The mellow motorman would enjoy a nineteen-year run of *Lunch with Casey* on "Track 11." During the mid-fifties, the station also featured *Captain 11* starring St. Paul native Jim Lange (who later would have the dubious distinction of hosting the ABC-TV show *The Dating Game*).

The on-screen fun and games of the local kids' shows masked a hardnosed ratings

Roger Awsumb as Casey Jones

Old Log's productions. He threw himself into his work, supervising every aspect from the acting to the lighting, often sleeping only when sheer exhaustion overtook him. Bob Aden remembered that more than once, snores drifted down from the rafters where Don had dozed off while setting the lights.

That fall, the fledgling theater company embarked on a road tour, which was originally planned to cover twenty-eight towns in Minnesota and North Dakota. One Sunday in early December, they were giving their matinee performance at the Mayo Civic Auditorium in Rochester, Minnesota, when news of the attack on Pearl Harbor came. The remainder of the tour was cancelled.

Don returned to Oklahoma to enlist in the U.S. Navy. The following summer he had not yet been called to active duty, so he returned to the Old Log for a second season of acting and directing. When the call from the navy still had not come by the fall of 1942, Don decided to try his luck in New York City. "I got work at CBS about two days after I arrived," he remembered. His career in the Big Apple was cut short, however. "Though work was coming in," Don declared, "I was very happy when, in December of that year, I received my orders from the Navy."

Don was sent to the Notre Dame Midshipman School, where he was commissioned as an ensign and retained as a navigation instructor. Around this time, he met a young woman named Joan Fuller, originally from South Bend, Indiana, who soon became his wife. Her knitting skills and innate artistic taste would be invaluable to her husband during the formative years of the Old Log, and for decades beyond. After leaving Notre Dame, Don was sent to the Pacific where he served as a navigator aboard the Fond Du Lac for two years and saw action at Okinawa and in Leyte Gulf. After the war, he was honorably discharged as a full lieutenant.

Soon after Don returned to civilian life in 1946, Harry Kuechle contacted him with the news that another group was interested in the Old Log building. If he wanted to revive the theater, he needed to catch a plane to Minnesota and sign a contract right away. Don called founder Bob Aden in Arizona to discuss what his plans for the theater were, if any. The end result was that Don bought the rights to the Old Log Theater for the tidy sum of one dollar.

Don's first season as owner of the Old Log may have left him won-

Don with two of his fans

dering if he had paid too much for the place. To begin with, his financial condition was so tenuous that he needed his father-in-law's credit just to buy a plane ticket to Minnesota. After the 1946 season got started, a polio epidemic kept many people at home – even the Minnesota State Fair was closed – so attendance at the theater was correspondingly anemic. To keep the enterprise going, Don was forced to sell virtually everything he owned, including his car. When the season finally ended, the Old Log had racked up a net loss of $7,000. Don hitch-hiked to California, where he scrounged around for roles in radio to sustain himself and his young family while he made plans for a comeback.

Figuring he had nowhere to go but up, Don returned the following summer for another season at the Old Log. It was still a struggle but a definite improvement over the year before, as the theater gradually built a following. In 1948, Don scored a public relations coup when he cast local newspapermen playing caricatures of themselves in his production of *The Front Page*.

Back then, the company typically would do thirteen different plays in thirteen weeks over the summer. In the off-season, Don would travel to New York or Los Angeles to find work in theater or radio. After about four years of this routine, a winter acting company in downtown Minneapolis became a possibility. Don was ready to settle down anyway, because the Stolz clan had been growing steadily. He remained in the Twin Cities that winter and, even though the new acting company didn't pan out, has stayed ever since.

While nurturing his struggling theater, Don did all sorts of jobs to make ends meet. He became a producer of trade shows, and a speech teacher for salesmen at Honeywell. He found work in local radio, which in the late 1940s still mounted productions that required actors. Long before he owned a TV set himself, he also got into the very young medium of television, doing production work at WTCN-TV for the advertising agency Campbell-Mithune, most notably commercials for Zinsmaster Bread. He and Brad Morris did a program called *The Weekly Review of the News*, with Don giving the weather reports.

It was during this time that he met Clellan Card, and the two quickly became friends. Don described Clellan as "a man with enormous sensitivity. He'd had two tragedies in his life, and as sometimes happens, instead of withdrawing from life – though he did at first – it made whatever he did richer, because he was more sensitive. Clellan was a marvelous man and an extraordinary talent. As I have told anyone who ever asked me, and a great many who didn't ask, he's the only handsome man I ever knew who had a gift for fantasy – and he probably had never used the word in his life. He had an extraordinary sense of what was funny, and what would appeal to kids."

Once the decision had been made to build a children's show around Axel, WCCO-TV's management assigned a staff director to the project, a reserved but affable young man named Harry Jones. He would make a number of important contributions to the new show.

Born in 1924 in Fall City, Nebraska, Harry Jones was the son of a traveling salesman, which kept the whole family on the move. Harry grew up in Kansas, Missouri, and Illinois, attending a different school nearly every year. The Joneses finally landed in Minneapolis just in time for Harry to graduate from Southwest High. He went on to the University of Minnesota for two years, but left to begin a career in journalism. The budding newspaperman soon found work as a reporter on the *Wichita Beacon* in Kansas. Any illusions that Harry may have had about the glamor of his chosen profession were quickly dispelled by his first assignment: compiling current prices at the stockyards every morning. Covering the police beat in the afternoons was only slightly more exciting. Before long, he returned to Minneapolis to explore other career possibilities.

He briefly worked in the promotion department of the *Minneapolis Star*, where he met Fran Blacklock and her husband, Les, an aspiring wildlife photographer. They became friends and decided to film a documentary on Isle Royale in Lake Superior. Before long, the three of them were trudging through the woods on the island, looking for moose. Each time they came upon their quarry, Harry's task as the

Say, what did you do when your wife smashed the car – bumper?

141

Harry Jones

"producer" was to outflank the animal and drive it towards the camera. Luckily, none of the beasts ever challenged his intentions. The sixteen-millimeter film that finally resulted, a combination travelogue and nature documentary, was called *Stalking the Royale Moose.*

Then a friend got Harry a job interview with station manager Sherm Headley at the newly created WTCN-TV. Using the Isle Royale film as his resumé, he managed to get a position in the film department at the station on April 18, 1949. "In fact, I *was* the film department," he recalled with a chuckle. The night the station first went on the air, Harry spent much of his time rewinding film, because – due to "technical difficulties" – 2600 feet of film had ended up on the floor.

In those nascent years of television, long before videotape, communications satellites, or even coaxial cable, local stations were scrambling to fill air time with any programming they could lay their hands on. Harry's main task at WTCN was to obtain feature films, short subjects, cartoons, and other material for the station to broadcast. The acquisition of film properties remained an important part of his job for quite some time, even after he became a director and producer of television shows such as *Soul's Harbor* and *Hi-Notes in Fashion.*

As its title implies, *Hi-Notes in Fashion* was a musical fashion program. First airing in 1952, each episode was built around a particular theme. Arle Haberle, WCCO-TV's women's activities director, hosted the proceedings and wrote the show's patter. She and Harry selected appropriate recordings and then choreographed the action to synchronize with the words and music. Every week the production boasted a stylish new set, created from little more than paper and paint by WCCO-TV staff artist Bill Dietrichson. All the frenzied

Did you like the apple – dumpling?

preparations finally culminated in a live studio broadcast every Friday night. The show was praised in the press as "unusual" with "a charming carefree style all its own."

By 1954, Harry had a wide range of experience in the still-young medium of television. He hadn't done any children's programming to speak of, but hardly anyone else had either, so he got the nod to do *Axel and His Dog*. In the years to come, Harry would helm most of WCCO-TV's children's programs.

Harry, Clellan, and Don worked out the basic premise of the Axel show, probably during the early summer of 1954. They all realized that visuals were crucial in the new medium of TV. Clellan had been doing Axel for years, but except for an occasional personal appearance, there hadn't been any need to concern himself with his alter ego's "look." On television, though, that would change. Axel needed a costume.

Most children's TV show characters fell into well-defined categories: cowboys, cops, clowns, superheroes, spacemen, sailors, train engineers, and the like. The one thing they all had in common was that their costumes were instantly recognizable even to very young children, providing a ready-made characterization. This shortcut method of acquiring a persona was attractive to many of the announcers, weathermen, and other television personnel who found themselves being pressed into service as video babysitters when the kidvid competition got hot.

Clellan didn't need to go that route; he was that rarity who already had a well-established character of his own creation. His challenge was to create a look for Axel that was funny and distinctive, and that somehow expressed the character's personality. He certainly succeeded; Axel's costume was simple yet memorable.

In fact, Axel was a man ahead of his time. Long before John, Paul, George, or Ringo had Beatle haircuts, Axel wore his hair combed forward in bangs, which was almost unheard of in the 1950s. A 1958 newspaper article described the surreptitious way that Axel's locks were trimmed: "When Clellan Card gets a haircut, he has the barber turn his chair around, quickly cut his front hair straight across, then turn the chair back so he's visible." On the show, Axel would frequently ruffle his fingers through his hair and ask with a self-satisfied air, "How do my curls look today?"

A bushy, reddish mustache erupted from beneath Axel's nose. At first of near-walrus proportions, within the first few months of the show it shrank to Chaplinesque size (perhaps to facilitate a greater range of facial expressions). With the smaller mustache, Axel vaguely resembled an idiotic Adolph Hitler, but apparently the similarity did not elicit any complaints from viewers.

Axel's vestments were every bit as distinguished as his tonsorial stylings. Despite his belief that a locomotive was "a crazy reason for doing something," he wore a train engineer's cap. In Axel's embryonic stage, the cap was worn in conventional fashion but later he habitually wore it high on the crown of his head with the brim sticking straight up.

On the earliest shows, Axel's striped shirt also differed from his classic look. At first it was a short-sleeved dress shirt with narrow vertical stripes, a collar, and buttons down the front. Before long, though, that was replaced by the quintessential Axel garment: a T-shirt with wide black-and-white horizontal stripes. A pair of broad suspenders held up Axel's baggy pants, and the vertical lines of his pale yellow suspenders contrasted nicely with the horizontal stripes of his shirt. To make absolutely sure that his pants stayed up, Axel added a long rope belt, and the ends dangled almost to his knees. He wore ordinary olive-green khakis for much of the show's run, but switched to blue satin trousers in the last years. Although his feet were rarely visible on the television screen, he sometimes wore tennis shoes laced up in quirky patterns.

Right from the very first program, there was another element that became as much a part of Axel's aura as his clothing: his magic spyglass. Allegedly a telescope, even a small child could see that Axel's spyglass was nothing more than two cardboard tubes, one nested inside the other. Originally painted cobalt blue, no color could hide the crudity of the prop. Yet somehow, the spyglass worked, probably because Axel so convincingly claimed that it did. He sometimes affectionately called it his flute and carefully put it away after each use, so that "nobody could steal it." He often talked about it as if it were the latest in modern technology, and spoke of turning up the "candlepower" to increase its range. Once, he claimed that he could see "even out to Esther Williams' house out to California out dere." The distances seemed to grow greater and greater as time went on,

I don't quite get your angle – worm!

until Axel declared that pretty soon he'd be able to look "clear around the world" and see into the end of his own spyglass!

The telescope worked beautifully as a transitional device. Every time Axel squinted into it, he directed the audience's attention to the next cartoon, short subject, or commercial. Though its appearance would change over the years, Axel's spyglass became an indelible part of his goofy gestalt from the moment he first peered through it.

One other aspect of the Axel character would be permanently established by the move to TV: his last name. In his original radio incarnation, Axel's surname had been *Swenson.* Sometime after Clellan left WCCO radio in 1944, that name was dropped in favor of Torgeson. Exactly when Axel got his new last name is unclear; it may have been when Clellan returned to WCCO radio in 1947, but it could have been as late as 1954. What is certain is that by the time that he arrived on television, he was Axel Torgeson – and would be forevermore.

The name of the new TV show, *Axel and His Dog*, pretty much summed up its contents. In its original conception, Axel and his

Axel and Towser on an early episode of *Axel and His Dog* in late 1954

dog, Towser, were the program's sole characters. Although Clellan probably named the mutt, it was Don Stolz who brought him to life. A canine of indeterminate breed, Towser was Axel's most trusted friend, and like any dog, he was loyal and eager to please. Although he couldn't speak in words, he definitely could communicate, using an amazing variety of barks, arfs, growls, howls, yips, yaps, and yelps. At times, it almost seemed as if Towser *could* talk.

In any case, Axel could always understand his faithful pooch. On one show, he asked Towser, "What aminal is the best timekeeper?" The dog uttered a staccato series of barks in reply. Axel shook his head, saying, "No, I think you have the wrong idea there. Try again, please." Towser barked again and Axel laughingly exclaimed, "Yah, he's right, a watch dog! Oh well, speaking of time, I s'pose that's the windup!"

While Clellan and Don created their memorable portrayals on-screen, Harry made his contributions behind the scenes. He conceived the setting: a ramshackle tree house atop a large tree in a forest. "My main philosophy, if you want to be artsy enough to call it that," he said modestly, "was that if you're going to do a kids' show, the setting is very important."

In retrospect, Harry's choice seems utterly perfect, a happy blend of reality and fantasy. To kids, a tree house offered a genuine refuge, a place where adults seldom ventured. Axel's Tree House was an idealized version of that childhood retreat, with the intimate atmosphere of a clubhouse. Anyone with a television set could join the gang. "It is entirely imaginative," Clellan declared in 1957. "We've put Axel, a crusty old guy who likes kids, in a tree house. It's a good setting for kids' imagination and lends itself to the stories I tell or the films being run."

Set designer Bill Dietrichson created the rustic environs of the tree house, which added much to the show's charm. Working with Harry on *Hi-Notes in Fashion*, he had become adept at conjuring cut-rate Babylonian gardens overnight, so creating a tree house in no time, at almost no cost, was no sweat. During the first few years of *Axel and His Dog*, the backdrops were painted with tempera on large sheets of seamless paper. This was economical, but somewhat impractical. The rigors of live TV demanded that the sets be put up and taken down in great haste during the short breaks between pro-

What's that on the wall – flour?

grams. This jostling tended to damage the fragile paper scenery, so that before long there were obvious creases.

The situation did have a fortunate by-product, however. Because the scenery was rendered unusable with some frequency, the talented Dietrichson was required to create a new background every few months, roughly in concert with the changing seasons. The different backgrounds gave Axel's Tree House a magical plasticity. The original décor featured serpentine, de Kooning-esque tree branches winding about an open-air porch, encircled by a rustic log fence. During the winter of 1954–1955, it was a cozy wood-paneled aerie enclosed by frosty windowpanes. The following summer it was an open-air porch again, and the sun-dappled leaves of the tree looked exuberantly colorful, even in black and white.

Director Jones' other major contribution to the show was his decree that Towser would remain unseen by the viewing audience, except for the dogs's large mottled brown paw. He disclaimed any originality in the idea, though.

"I saw a kinescope [a television program filmed from a TV monitor] of a show that Soupy Sales was doing, I think in Detroit. He would stand in the doorway and talk with something beyond the doorway. As I recall, he would look up as if this was some enormously tall monster, or whatever, of some kind. And not being able to see it was the thing that intrigued me. I figured that if you really saw Towser, all you'd see was some kind of a dumb dog outfit that would never convince anybody. I always felt very strongly that kids liked that kind of imagination. I mean, what did Towser really look like? Well, we never *ever* showed Towser on the air."

The only part of Towser that viewers did see was his huge brown paw, marbleized with white streaks, which was actually a sort of gigantic mitten that fit over Don's entire arm. On the show, that furry forefoot usually seemed to be in perpetual motion. Perhaps to compensate for his limited vocabulary, Towser was quite physical. He would often reach over to Axel and pat him on the shoulder, pull down a suspender, bop him on the head, or even pinch his nether regions. No matter how rough things got, though, there was never any doubt about the genuine affection that existed between Axel and his dog, which reflected the real friendship between Clellan and Don.

Unlike many kids' TV shows, *Axel and His Dog* did not include a "peanut gallery" full of breathless, restless youngsters. Clellan, Don, and Harry all felt that seeing the show in the studio would shatter the illusion for kids. Watching Axel cavort in black and white on the screen at home might seem magical, but seeing the same thing in person might expose him as a man in a goofy costume in front of a cheap painted backdrop. Worse, it would be impossible to prevent a studio audience from seeing Don, so Towser's true appearance would be revealed as well. That could never be allowed to happen. Despite the silliness, *Axel and His Dog* always maintained a tantalizing air of mystery.

Like virtually all local kids' programs of the era, Axel's show followed a "wraparound" format: the live sequences with the local host were wrapped around pre-recorded material, usually cartoons or short comedy films. There were two primary reasons why the wraparound format was the dominant form of local kidvid all across the country. The first was economic: it was far cheaper to fill air time with filmed segments than to hire a staff to create hours of original entertainment every day. The second reason was the sheer difficulty of holding the attention of juvenile viewers. The cartoons and film shorts added variety. Even in the relatively sedate 1950s, things had to keep moving. Few performers were capable of mesmerizing an audience of children for a solid half-hour, day in and day out.

But why bother with a host at all? Why not simply run pre-recorded material exclusively? Because using kiddie emcees did have its advantages. Distinctive characters helped create the station's identity, and differentiated it from the competition. Moreover, the characters could go out on personal appearances and generate additional publicity and goodwill. Most importantly, sponsors loved them. When Axel or one of his compatriots pitched merchandise, kids listened – and then pestered their parents to purchase the product.

Once the films had been lined up, Axel's costume had been prepared, Towser's paw had been sewn, and the set had been constructed and painted, suddenly it was time for the premiere. Like virtually all television programs of the era, it would be broadcast live. Cast and crew had a quick run-through to determine the basic positions for the two floor cameras, but it really wasn't a proper rehearsal. There was no script – the show was always basically ad-libbed.

Another photo of the premiere episode of *Axel and His Dog*
(notice Don behind the original foreground tree trunk)

At 5:00 P.M. on Thursday, August 5, 1954, Axel Torgeson greeted the television viewing audience for the first time. According to Don Stolz, it nearly turned out to be the last time as well. WCCO-TV had been running promotional announcements for the program during the summer, inviting kids to send in jokes for Axel to read over the air. This had netted a stack of postcards chock-full of gags, knock-knocks, and riddles. The first show had proceeded pretty smoothly, despite the usual hectic atmosphere off-camera – until Axel decided that it was time to read some of those jokes that the kids had sent in.

Plucking a letter from the pile, he read aloud: "Why does the chicken cross the road?" Perhaps chuckling at the notion that the first joke on his new program would be the world's oldest chestnut, Axel read the punch line before he realized what he was saying: "Because she's laying the farmer on the other side!"[15]

What are we having for dinner, chicken – dumplings?

Mary Davies as Carmen the Nurse

Even when confronted with the most ancient chestnuts, the silly Scandinavian bubbled with infectious laughter, and often embellished them with his own absurdities. On one show, in response to the riddle "Name three collective nouns," Tallulah shouted, "I know! Fly paper, the garbage can, and Axel."

"Fly paper, the garbage can, and Ax – hey!" Axel yelped. He suddenly assumed a serious expression. "See that my name never gets connected with them refuses things, like garbage and stuff," he ordered gravely. "No – I don't think the garbage people would like it!" He chuckled, "Well, I remember when me and Tallulah was workin' on a garbage truck, you know – fifteen dollars a week and all we could eat! I think I've aten the most! Ha-ha-ha! Wow, am I slingin' 'em fast today, boy!"

Clellan and Don soon developed a running gag with the mail. Often, when either Towser or Tallulah would hand over a letter, they'd hold it right in front of Axel's face, blocking him from view, much to his annoyance. "As I've always said," he admonished Towser one day, "don't hold the mail in front of my physissiognomy, see, because it prewents me from looking out into the vast multitude what might be assembled in the forest." On another show, Axel gave an additional reason for his objection. "We have complaints from the ladies in the audience when you cover up my face," he claimed. "They say they're missing half the enjoyment of looking at me here in the tree house."

Despite occasional disappointment among his female fans, Mr. Torgeson began to build an audience. At first, *Axel and His Dog* was broadcast just one day a week, but by September 6 the show's frequency was increased to three days per week. The following month, it began running every weekday at 5:30 P.M. Ratings were not high, but WCCO was willing to give the new show a chance to prove itself.

As a matter of fact, *Axel and His Dog* had been on the air for only two months when it was selected for a singular honor: it would be the first Twin Cities television show broadcast in color. Although KSTP-TV had telecast some network color programming earlier, *Axel and His Dog* would be the very first such show to originate locally, albeit as an experiment. The colorcast was the culmination of months of work. The complex color television equipment, purchased by WCCO

Stagehand Ray Hurd, Clellan, Don, Harry, and
set designer Bill Dietrichson on October 8, 1954

for nearly $250,000, had arrived at the station in July. New rack space
had to be added in the control room for the bulky appurtenances,
in order to properly segregate the black-and-white and color opera-
tions. In addition to color TV programs on the CBS network and in
closed circuit demonstrations, over the summer WCCO thoughtfully
provided its viewers with "a regularly scheduled 30-minute color-bar
test pattern each Saturday morning."

Set designer Bill Dietrichson constructed a colorful new tree
house set expressly for the distinctive broadcast, mainly because
Axel's regular set was painted in blacks, whites, and grays. Unlike
the stagy and two-dimensional everyday tree house, the polychrome
version was decorated with real tree branches, the leaves in red and
brown autumn hues. The blue sky of the backdrop shimmered with
wispy cirrus clouds. Live parrots and other variegated birds in cages,
courtesy of local pet stores, were placed around the stage to provide
additional eye-catching window dressing.

On Friday, October 8, 1954, at 5:30 P.M., the special show was
introduced with these words: "The program you are about to see
marks another milestone in Twin Cities television. It will be the first

full-color telecast to originate in any local studio. Those of you with color television sets will see *Axel and His Dog* today in glowing natural color. Others will see the same program in rich black and white." Because his usual striped shirt didn't offer much pizzazz to the handful of viewers with color sets, Axel wore a bright red, long-sleeved undershirt just for the occasion. Those few who were privileged to see the show in color also might have noticed that Axel's bushy mustache was considerably redder than his hair. During the broadcast itself Axel, Towser, and Tallulah carried on pretty much as they always did: joking, poking, and provoking each other.

Ironically, that very first Twin Cities colorcast was the *only* occasion when *Axel and His Dog* was broadcast in color. By the time that WCCO-TV began telecasting all of its programming in full color – on election night in November 1966 – Axel was off the air forever.

About a week after Axel's color premiere, a crisis arose that would have long-lasting repercussions. Clellan was seized with a serious coughing fit, perhaps due to his chronic allergies, and he hacked so hard for so long that he ruptured a blood vessel on a vocal cord. To

Don and Clellan during the color broadcast on October 8, 1954

What did you do when you sat on the bed – spring?

allow the rupture enough time to heal, his doctor advised him not to talk for several weeks. For a man in the broadcasting profession, that was not welcome news.

Perhaps most disappointing for Clellan, he would be unable to participate in WCCO radio's thirtieth anniversary program on Thursday, October 21. A live re-creation of *Almanac of the Air* had been planned as part of the extravaganza, but in light of Clellan's condition, that portion of the show was cancelled.

Clellan's illness also created a pressing problem for director Harry Jones: producing a live television show when the star was unable to talk. Obviously, a substitute was required, but there was no time to hold auditions or comb through resumés; Harry needed an experienced pro, and fast. He called a young woman whom both he and Clellan had worked with many times before: singer and entertainer Mary Davies.

One of six children, Mary seemed destined for a musical career almost from the day she was born, on June 26, 1925. Her father was a professor of German and the *Minneapolis Tribune* music critic for thirty years, and he enjoyed playing bridge with a certain Dr. William Card. Her mother was a violinist who took up the newspaper column when her husband died in 1940. Years later, Mary described her own introduction to performing: "At the age of four I started right up there at the top of the heap with the Chicago Opera Company. My first brush with a stage was at the Minneapolis Auditorium as 'Little Trouble' in *Madame Butterfly*. This was quite a noteworthy send-off with great amounts of publicity. It also infected my system with the desire to be near a stage and music and performing, which has carried over into these advanced years."

Mary attended Central High School, and later majored in speech at the University of Minnesota. She studied voice and classical music, but her ambition was to be a pop singer. During World War II, she often sang at university functions and for the USO. Those gigs eventually led to an audition with Bud Strawn's Orchestra. Mary got the job, but it was hardly a dream come true. She remembered it as "the most tortuous, tortured few years of my life – I just couldn't stand it." However distasteful it may have been, the job was a springboard to better things. One day in about 1946, the band made an appearance on a WTCN radio program called *The Dayton's Soda Set Show*, which besides, Clellan already had a very capable co-star in Don Stolz.

In addition to incontinent skunks, Axel's Tree House was often visited by other "aminals" (as he called them), some on more than a one-shot basis. Many of them appeared courtesy of the Uptown Pet "Hotel" in Minneapolis. Two semi-regulars during the first year of the show were Sylvia the monkey and Hazel the burro.

Sylvia was a spider monkey, a South American variety equipped with a prehensile tail. For several months, she attained

Axel and Sylvia the monkey

what amounted to co-star status on the show, treated as Towser and Tallulah's equal in early promotional material, as well as appearing in the color telecast. Axel treated her indulgently, although she had to endure the indignity of wearing baby clothes. During Sylvia's visits, he would talk to her, offer her a peek through his spyglass, or dance around the set with her in his arms. One day, he showed Sylvia a letter and asked her who it was from. When he pretended that she answered, Tallulah said with disdain, "Don't be silly. Who ever heard of a monkey that could read?"

"Who ever heard of a monkey what could read?" Axel cried, and then stage-whispered to the audience, "Who ever heard of a pewsy-cat what could talk?"

Beginning in January 1955, Hazel Hernandez the burro was trotted out periodically. Allegedly from Mexico, she was a small "Biblical" donkey, so-called because perpendicular lines on her back resembled a cross – although Axel claimed that she looked "kind of like my bruder-in-law." On one show, Hazel licked Axel's fingers so assiduously that she seemed to be trying to swallow them. He assured the kids at home, "She's so gentle you can pewt your whole hand right in her mouth and she don't bite it off or nothin' – at least not yet!"

Off-camera, Hazel was stabled in Excelsior, which meant that Don

Axel and Hazel the burro

had to transport her to the studio. "I would have to load that damn burro in the station wagon and drive into town with it," he remembered ruefully.

The use of live animals as regulars on *Axel and His Dog* was probably doomed from the outset. Neither monkeys nor burros take direction very well. There were times when Sylvia was clearly frightened by the strange goings-on on the set, and she reacted by screeching loudly. Like the skunk that Carmen had encountered, Hazel had the disconcerting habit of occasionally relieving herself in the studio, which didn't exactly enhance the working environment. Sylvia and Hazel ultimately were more trouble than they were worth, so they were eased out of the show before the end of 1955.

Just after Christmas in 1954, Clellan appeared on television in color again (at least to the sprinkling of viewers who had the sets), this time on a special called *Country Holiday*. Most of the Axel gang was on board as well: Mary Davies co-starred and Harry Jones directed. The show, described in publicity as a "sophisticated rural scene," also featured the Mickrae Dancers of Minneapolis and the music of the Red River Valley Gang, led by violinist Bill Metchnek.

He always spoke directly to his young viewers, reading letters, spinning yarns, and pitching products. Other kiddie show hosts did the same sorts of things, but few had Axel's verve (or nerve!). Most tried to be "good role models," but by avoiding any hint of human flaws, they tended to create bloodless characters who seemed more like cardboard cut-outs than people. Even children could see them for what they were: grown-ups in silly costumes.

Not Axel. Despite his goofy get-up and odd speech, he seemed real, with a well-defined personality that included plenty of faults and foibles. He could be argumentative, vain, or just plain stupid, but most of the time he also seemed to be enjoying himself immensely. Kids could identify with him; he was obviously an adult, but it was equally apparent that he hadn't forgotten what it was like to be young. Axel wasn't afraid to appear ridiculous by acting nutty or making faces. Promotion director Tom Cousins recalled, "He could cross his eyes like nobody I've ever seen!"

Clellan's kidvid role seemed to re-energize him. He told his favor-

Axel and Towser promoting Woodnik toys

ite old jokes, but with a new enthusiasm. He gave his imagination free rein, indulging in funny flights of fancy or barbed in-jokes as the mood struck him. Axel was so gleefully, impudently unrestrained, it almost seemed as if the old Scandihoovian had sprung from Clellan's id.

One aspect of the character that struck every viewer immediately was the peculiar way he spoke. On radio, his accent had originally been Swedish, but over the years it evolved into a less-clearly defined patois. The transformation was supposedly hastened by a couple of talks with the Swedish consul, who – unlike most of the broadcast audience – took a dim view of Clell's lampooning. There were a few others who were not amused either. Some conscientious parents and teachers, trying to teach their children proper English, were appalled by Axel's speech. "We had objections to the fracturing of the English language," Harry recalled. "We ended up having some rather serious discussions at the station about that. However, I think that Clell was wise enough to realize that if he cleaned it up, the character went. I would agree now; in retrospect, I just don't see how he could have maintained the character."

Clellan occasionally satirized the controversy on the show itself. One Sunday morning, Axel greeted his young audience with some florid prose and then turned to Tallulah and said, "Listen to my grammar this morning. Ain't it beautiful?"

"Very nice," Tallulah agreed.

"Yes, I'm glad," Axel declared. "You know, Tallulah is sort of my tutor, and she sees that I don't say nothin' that ain't wrotten down on the paper."

"Anything that isn't written," corrected Tallulah.

"'That isn't written,'" Axel repeated. "I see. Well, all right, I'll be very careful to say 'isn't written.' All right, I'm sittin' down and I'm written a letter to my friend. Is that all right to say?"

"No!" Tallulah wailed.

Axel tried again: "Wrotten a letter!"

Almost tearfully, Tallulah meowed, "No!"

"Wrot!" Axel barked in desperation.

"Yes, you have," Tallulah sighed.

Axel's grammar was certainly atrocious, liberally strewn with "ain'ts," double negatives, and other errors. His diction was equally

Don as Tallulah and Axel at the crotch of the tree

The show really began to hit its stride: all the classic elements were in place, but everything was still fresh. Early on, Axel had seemed a bit more like a typical TV "uncle host," excitedly gushing and babbling about anything. While never condescending, during the first year of the show he sometimes seemed overeager, laying on the charm a little too thick. He gradually grew more comfortable in his role as a kiddie guru, and his easygoing affability evolved into an impish nonchalance, a jocular – almost sardonic – sang-froid. But he always had a natural ability to connect with his young audience.

Meanwhile, Tallulah developed into a hairy harridan. The cordial relationship that she and Axel at first had enjoyed evaporated, replaced by almost constant complaints, squabbles, and feuds. They traded verbal parries with abandon, to the delight of viewers.

Luckily enough, a series of programs were filmed at this point, preserving *Axel and His Dog* at its peak. In fact, over eighty episodes are extant, far more than remain of most local children's television programs of the era, thanks to a fortuitous chain of events. As the show became more and more popular, it aired more and more frequently. When it premiered in August 1954, it ran only on Thursdays; the schedule gradually increased until by the following April, the show was on seven days a week. Clellan and Don, not unreasonably, wanted some time off so the station offered to pre-record the Sunday shows on 16mm film (videotape not yet being available). On three Saturdays in March 1955, the idea was given a trial run with Don Pottratz, the head of WCCO-TV's photographic department, as the cinematographer. Results were good, so filming Axel's Sunday segments began.

From April 1955 to September 1956, on Thursday afternoons the cast and crew shot Axel's "ins and outs" (so-called because they led into and out of other material) for broadcast on Sunday. As an incidental by-product of this process, the programs were preserved. In those days, most local television shows were performed live and not recorded at all. When videotape came into use, the expensive tape was used over and over again, each time erasing the previously recorded programs. Film, however, is more permanent. The episodes of *Axel and His Dog* that were committed to celluloid were there for good.

WCCO-TV film editor Claude Heisch (left) and Harry Jones

But that would have been of no avail if the films had been thrown out — and indeed, over the years a lot of other footage has been lost. Fortunately, WCCO-TV's film editor Claude Heisch took it upon himself to protect the station's legacy of programs. It was an uphill battle at times, but he managed to preserve a selection of WCCO-TV's early programming, including approximately eight hours of *Axel and His Dog*.

Most of the surviving programs are somewhat atypical, however. Because more than 90 percent of the filmed episodes originally aired on Sundays, Axel often began them by encouraging kids to go to church or Sunday School (once he said that "everybody" starts out Sunday that way). These were undoubtedly sincere statements from Clellan Card, a practicing Catholic, but they might give unenlightened viewers the impression that church was a regular topic on the show. Nothing could be further from the truth.

The Sunday shows were relatively free of commercials, too, which was decidedly not the case for those that aired Monday through Saturday. Few weekday programs exist, but those that do are a striking contrast to the relatively placid Sabbath episodes; some are little more than wall-to-wall advertisements. The popular program attracted both local and national advertisers, and over the years Axel pushed a huge variety of products. Some are still well known today while others have been utterly forgotten. Clover Leaf Milk, Peters Weiners, Crystal Sugar, Kemps/Crescent Ice Cream, the Trading Post–Skate Exchange, Hostess Cupcakes, Chicken Dinner and Denver Sandwich Candy Bars, Smith Brothers Cough Drops, Magic Milk Shake, Eveready Cocoa, Wag Dog Food, Nabisco Cereals, Instant Mello Crunch Dog Food, Billy Boy Jams and Jellies, Canada Dry Ginger Ale, Woodnik Toys, Pop Drops, Fanny Farmer Candy, Poll-Parrot Shoes, Cadbury's Candy Bars, Holsum Bread, and Tonka Toys were just a few of the show's sponsors.

Axel, like Clellan, was a very effective pitchman. He had a funny way of getting viewers involved. For one Malt-o-Meal commercial, he carefully prepared a heaping bowlful of the hot cereal, adding lots of sugar and cream. "Boy, wouldn't you like to wrap yourself around that?" he asked excitedly. "Man, I'd like to dive into it myself right now!" Actually, it wasn't unusual for a significant portion of a food display to disappear down the gullets of the crew.

Sponsors' wares often inspired practical jokes as well. The stagehands loved to doctor product samples to rattle Axel during the commercials, which – like the rest of the show – were done live with

Axel with a display of Fanny Farmer Easter candy

no possibility of retakes. On one show, they prepared a glass of Fizzies (effervescent flavored tablets) with hot water instead of cold. On-camera, Axel took a gulp, nearly gagged, and then proclaimed, "It's even good warm!"

Life on the set of *Axel and His Dog* settled into a pleasant routine. Clellan and Don would usually get to the studio about fifteen minutes before showtime, although sometimes they would cut it even closer. The two actors and their director would briefly discuss the plan for the day's show, usually concentrating on the commercials. Cardboard cue sheets, about two by three feet in size, were prepared and propped up on a large easel out of camera range. One for each in-and-out segment, they didn't contain much dialogue. Don noted, "There might not be a word there except the lead-in to the film, how Axel was going to lead into the first section of film." The cue sheets contained information about current contests, sponsor names, slogans, and other details such as product flavors, free prizes, or an item's special features. If the client or the product were new, the com-

What did you have for dessert, Tutti – Frutti?

mercial would actually be rehearsed, usually while one of the sections of film was running. Even so, Don rarely had to learn any lines. Mostly he just reacted to whatever Clellan did.

Although the ads were rehearsed at least some of the time, the rest of the show was ad-libbed from beginning to end. There never was a script – except once. The story goes that one day Clellan phoned Don and asked him, "Have you looked at the ratings?" Don didn't ever check the ratings; he knew that the show was one of the most popular in the Twin Cities and didn't care to delve any deeper than that. Cagily, he told Clellan, "Well, no, I haven't seen them yet."

Clellan said gravely, "We're down."

When asked how much the show's ratings had declined, Clell responded that they had dropped a point or so. "That isn't much," Don said. "It shouldn't worry you."

"Well, it does," Clellan insisted. "I think we should do something about it, so I've written a script and I think we should come in early to rehearse it. Harry's going to be there, and we'll all go through the script together."

"How early should I come in?" Don asked.

In all seriousness, Clellan replied, "Oh, fifteen minutes."

When Don got to the studio, Harry was there already – he was always there, it seemed – but Clellan had not yet arrived. They waited and waited, and finally he came in, just a few minutes before the show was scheduled to start.

"All right, where's this script of yours?" Don said skeptically.

"Yes, I'd like to see it, too," seconded Harry.

Clell pulled a small scrap of paper, perhaps two by three inches, out of his pocket and announced, "Here it is." He held it up and pointed to the notes scribbled there. "Now, look – I'll say this line first, and you say that line, then I'll say this, and then we'll fool around a little bit, and then go into the first section of film. After that, I'll come back out and – well, we can go through that during the film." So much for the one and only script!

As Don well knew, there really wasn't any need for written dialogue; he and Clellan could improvise a routine at the drop of a line. "Say, a funny thing happened to me on the way to the tree house today," Axel began one morning. "Over to that little ice cream store, you know, down to the crossroads in the forest. So I go in there and I set down and I say to the squirt there, the soda squirt, I say, 'I would like anything but chocolate,' see?

"And so the fella looks at me and he says, 'Yeah, Axel, we can fix you up. We happen to be out of chocolate, though.' So I says, 'Give me anything but wanilla.' And he says, 'Well, we're clean out of wanilla.' And so I took a banana split!"

"That *was* funny," Tallulah said sarcastically.

"It depends on the flavors of the banana split," the nutty Norseman retorted. "Tallulah's making funny faces over dere. Or aren't you? It's just your natural face hanging there, huh? Take the mask off, Tallool!"

A bit later, Axel returned to the subject of his banana split. "You know, she says to me, 'What did you do after you ate the banana – split?' Like that, see? She's makin' up Birdies for me down dere. That's why I had the banana split, to give her the oppertunity."

"Oh, and that was funny," Tallulah remarked dubiously.

"Yeah, dat was wery, wery funny down dere," he claimed.

The cat responded caustically, "If I'd known that, I could have laughed."

Axel's patience abruptly ran out. "You could've laughed but – why don't you, instead of monkeying around like you're doing and wasting time," he snapped, "give me some mail because I can get much more accomplished without your trying to make funnies over dere, just because you happen to be hopped up with a little catnip today and overdosed."

In reply, Tallulah gave him a raspberry. Axel stared woefully at the camera for a moment, then turned back to the cat. "Please, no opinions here," he requested. "It's your natural noise, all right – I'll say that."

Axel and His Dog was freewheeling and spontaneous, but that didn't mean that the principals didn't care about what they were doing. "People, I know, thought that Clellan was haphazard and lackadaisical, but he was very serious about it," Don asserted. "And he was terribly aware of what the show meant to youngsters and he felt a tremendous responsibility." Their peers in the broadcasting industry recognized Clellan's contribution. On April 27, 1955, Clellan was named "Best Children's Show Personality" by the Minneapolis Ad Club and the Twin Cities chapter of the American Federation of Tele-

A SUMMER'S DAY IN AUGUST, 1955

Another perfect morning at the lake with the sun shining and a whole day of fun ahead!

First, I'll hurry down to the theater and see what the actors are doing, then maybe Peter and Dony will let me ride into Excelsior with them on our bikes. We could stop at the Amusement Park for a ride on the merry-go-round, then head into the Ben Franklin – I wanna buy a pea shooter. Then I'll come home for lunch before sailing with the Kimball boys. (I hope they don't tip it … the lake looks scary today.) Then hurry downtown with Daddy to the studio. Axel said he'd read Dony's joke on TV today.

A perfect day! Mom even has sweet rolls for breakfast. And look, little Joannie is up already. "Joannie, can you say 'perfect day'? I can't believe how much you can talk. All right, Joannie, I'll give you some of my sweet roll, but first you have to give me a kiss. That was a good one. Bye-bye."

Oh, little Joannie, why didn't I give you your bite of sweet roll? Your kiss is stolen property … and now I can't give it back.

Clellan, no stranger to that sort of grief, did what he could to console his colleague, and their mutual tragedies cemented their friendship on a deep level. "No one ever had a better friend," Don said emphatically. The following New Year's Eve, Clellan and Marion invited Don and his wife, Joan, to their home, where they commiserated in their profound sorrow. "It was an enormously sad but wonderful night," Don recalled, his voice choking. "Clellan was a good man."

A 1957 map of Magic Island

revealed in more detail as well. The area had been vaguely defined at first, just a bucolic woodland where the Little Rascals frolicked. But by the summer of 1957, it had been established that the tree house existed in a mythical place called Magic Island. That fanciful isle became the locale for all of Channel 4's growing list of children's shows: *Johnny .44!*, with Jack Hastings as a cowboy at the Lucky Horse Shoe Ranch; *Popeye's Club House*, featuring unlikely sailor Mel Jass (until Mel joined WTCN-TV that July, and was replaced by Dale Woodley); and *Commodore Cappy*, starring John Gallos as a nautical geezer who piloted an atomic submarine, and who sounded like a cross between Lionel Barrymore and "Walter Brennan in heat," according to Gallos.

Since *Commodore Cappy* and *Axel and His Dog* were aired back to back, it wasn't difficult to persuade Don Stolz to handle the puppets on *Cappy* as well. Don had to make the long drive from Excelsior every day to do the Axel gig anyway; getting paid to do another program made the trip more worthwhile. John Gallos was always quick to credit Don for making *Commodore Cappy* a hit. "The reason it became very successful in a short period of time was I had as my puppeteer Don Stolz," he declared generously.

Don certainly had a hand in the success of *Axel and His Dog* as well. It's true that nothing much ever really *happened* in the tree house; one episode was pretty much like another. Viewers enjoyed it because Clellan and Don had fun, and that came across on-screen.

They could conjure mirth out of the thinnest premise. One Sunday, for example, Axel did battle with Towser and Tallulah in an epic tic-tac-toe contest. During his game with the dog, Axel bragged, "Oh, diss iss easy. I could win diss game thinkin' about somethin' else wid my left foot off the ground."

After Towser marked his second *X*, Axel whispered confidentially to the audience, "I'm gonna sneak a fast one on him and if I get diss udder corner, then I get two adwantages, both approaching from da north, and one from da south, see? One if by land and one if by sea, see? I'll pewt diss mark right here, see? And then I'll get to him quick." He then laboriously put an *O* in a square that failed to block a win for *X*.

The dog quickly put his final mark on the board, drew a line through his row of *X*s, and made a yelping hiccup sound – evidently

What did you do when you went to the zoo with your aunt – eater?

Axel with his spyglass

canine laughter. "Towser, for da cat's sake! Now look – you scheated!" Axel complained. "You pewt two *X*s dere where you weren't s'posed to pewt 'em! I wasn't lookin'! I was talkin' to da kids! You scheated, Towser! I'm goin' to call da police! I'm *not* going to stand fer diss!" With that, Axel imperiously plucked his spyglass from its perch and looked down into the forest.

Later in the program, the bizarre feline yodeling of Tallulah was heard. "Oh! Here comes Tallulah!" Axel exclaimed. "Say, I'm gonna play dat game wit' Tallulah and beat Tallulah to a pulp! Nobody like Towser gonna be around doin' no scheatin'." Then, with elaborate

  What's the trouble with the baby-buggy?

promoted the addition of the *Little Lulu*, *Puppetoon*, *Noveltune*, and *Color Classics* cartoons to the *Axel and His Dog* program, and a change in Axel's time slot. The station was inundated with drawings.

Some prizes were modest. A December 1955 contest from the Trading Post–Skate Exchange dangled Pinocchio dolls as rewards for kids who completed the sentence, "I would like skates for Christmas because ..." Other awards were more spectacular. The Crystal Sugar Colorama Contest sweetened the summer of 1955 for six weeks. The first, second, and third place winners were each awarded a sporty pedal car. The lucky first-place winner also got a Dodge Lancer – a *real* car.

A kid-size train was the big prize in the summer of 1958. Headed by an engine large enough for a young engineer to comfortably ride on, it could chug around a backyard on its own track with a line of kiddie boxcars trailing behind. In May, 1959, the "Sugar Specs Special," a gas-powered quarter midget racer, drove the Wheaties–Sugar Specs Contest. Viewers were asked to name the twins on the Sugar Specs cereal box, and to include one box top from Wheaties and one from Sugar Specs with each entry. Axel gave away a Schwinn bike, an RCA phonograph, and five pairs of roller skates each week until August, when all entrants had a chance to win the midget racer grand prize.

In those early, free-wheeling days of TV, contests sometimes could be quite impromptu. One day in April, 1956, when Towser grew particularly rambunctious, Axel exclaimed, "Don't scare me like dat! Diss dog comes leapin' at me and wants to set in my lap alla time. He's only about umpteen feet tall, ya know." This last remark sparked an idea. "Say, I think it would be nice if the kids would send us some pitchers of what they think you look like, hah? I'd sure like ta know what the kids think you look like, Towser. Maybe the boys should draw what they think Towser looks like and the girls should draw what they think Tallulah looks like." No prize was offered, but no doubt kids sent in their sketches anyway.

Don fondly recalled another contest that was improvised on the spur of the moment one cold Minnesota day. During a break in the show, Clellan suddenly turned to him and said, "Boy, I'd love some good fudge right now, wouldn't you?" "Yeah, that does sound good," Don agreed. When they went back on the air, Axel impulsively

What would you do if she swiped the salt – shaker?

Axel and the newly-hatched Malty the Breakfast Bird

announced a fudge contest. He volunteered ten dollars of his own money as the prize for the best batch. According to Don, "hundreds of pounds" of fudge flooded the station in response. Judge Torgeson chose a winner – based on extensive taste tests, no doubt – and then most of the candy was given to hospitals, nursing homes, and charitable institutions. In that more innocent era, no one had any qualms about distributing so much food prepared by so many diverse hands. The notion that any of it could be less than wholesome never entered anyone's mind.

Sometimes Axel had help in these commercial endeavors. During 1956, Malty the Breakfast Bird regularly popped up in a five-minute segment called "Watch the Birdie." During this portion of the show, Axel called a local child who had sent in his or her name on the back of a Malt-o-Meal box top, and asked the question which had just appeared on the TV screen. A correct answer won a prize. Created by WCCO-TV staffer Wally Green and the Art Department of the Campbell-Mithun advertising agency, Malty was a goggle-eyed avian who resembled Woody Woodpecker with a nose job. In reality, of course, it was another hand puppet manipulated by Don Stolz.

sters to Axel Day were distributed through food and drug stores, and other sponsors connected with WCCO-Television Merchandising. The tickets weren't actually necessary for admission; they were really just advertisements for the extravaganza.

A planned parade of "Junior Axels" and doll buggies provided a peg on which Channel 4 personalities could hang Axel Day promotions. Far in advance of the big day, costumed boys and buggy-pushing girls were invited to appear as guests on various WCCO-TV programs. During the week preceding the celebration, all of Channel 4's children's personalities hammered away about the upcoming event.

The station also ballyhooed the happening with on-air promos: "Boys and girls! Don't forget! Next Saturday is AXEL DAY AT EXCEL-SIOR PARK! There'll be a big show, prizes, and free rides for everyone! Old Axel will be there looking for you, along with his friends, Commodore Cappy, Johnny .44, and Mel Jass. So get Mother or Dad to bring you out to AXEL DAY AT EXCELSIOR PARK! The gates open at noon next Saturday."

Every sponsor who had two or more spots on *Axel and His Dog*, *Bugs Bunny Time*, *Johnny .44!*, or *Popeye's Club House* was invited to participate in the Axel Day promotion free of charge. Flav-r Straws, Holsum Bread, Nabisco Cereals, Canada Dry, and Hi-C Orange Drink signed up.

For taking part, each sponsor was given:

1) booth space which could be decorated with point-of-sale or other product promotion material;

2) a listing on some of the 400,000 tickets that were distributed, plus a generous supply of tickets to distribute themselves;

3) identification with specific Channel 4 "kid show" personalities, who used sponsors' booths as "autograph party headquarters" at specified times;

4) the opportunity to stage various promotional stunts with a large and enthusiastic crowd, such as free sample distribution, small merchandise prizes, and participation in the Pavilion Show; and

5) the opportunity to offer additional chances for prizes in exchange for labels from their products.

As if that weren't enough, kids could also enter the Axel Day photo contest. The ten best photographs snapped at Excelsior Park would win five dollars each. Any prize-winning photo that included Axel, Commodore Cappy, Johnny .44, or Mel Jass would be awarded double the usual amount, ten whole dollars! Still more prizes were awarded simply for showing up. Every youngster who attended the 1957 Axel Day was given a ticket which might win a prize in the big drawing. Kids could increase their chances of winning by obtaining special tickets distributed in grocery stores or by saving sponsors' product labels, which they could trade for extra tickets in the drawing when they arrived at Excelsior Park.

A staggering array of more than seven hundred toys, worth in excess of $2,000, would be offered in the big drawing:

    12 – 15" Honeysuckle Dolls
    12 – 19" Honeysuckle Dolls
    12 – 17" Honeybunch Dolls with hat and coat
    12 – Betsy Wetsy Dolls with layette
    12 – Deluxe Betsy Wetsy Dolls in case
    12 – 18" Kissing Pink Dolls
     3 – 21" Cherries a La Mode Dolls
    12 – 18" Queen of Diamond Dolls
    24 – Snoozie Dolls in blankets
    18 – J. Fred Muggs Dolls
    12 – Fixit Tow Trucks and Cars
    24 – Dragnet Police Cars
    18 – XP 600 Fixit Cars
     8 – Fire Engines
    36 – Autorama Cars
     6 – Roy Rogers' Stage Coaches
     6 – Roy Rogers' Chuck Wagons
    12 – Robot Bulldozers
    12 – Mobile Rocket Launchers
     6 – Turbo-Jet Rockets
    12 – Knights on Horses
    12 – Riders on Horses
    24 – Hopalong Cassidy & Topper
    36 – Toy Mechanical Shavers
    36 – Robert the Robot
    12 – Mickey Mouse Race
    24 – Badminton Sets

36 – Whirl-a-Bubble
12 – Talking Telephone Banks
12 – Russell Wright Am MDN
36 – Boat Firefighters
36 – Mechanical Speedboats
12 – Salvage Boats with divers
12 – 21" Power Speedboats
36 – Launch Takapart
24 – Sparkling Boats
24 – Racing Boats
36 – Mickey Mouse Sailing Vessels

The big day finally arrived. The gates of Excelsior Amusement Park were thrown open at noon, and the hordes descended. Axel arrived in his "antique automobile," a tin lizzie not unlike the car that Clellan had been given by his father more than thirty years before.

The first event of the day was the parade of doll buggies and "Junior Axels." Participants had been pre-selected, based on snapshots which they had mailed to Channel 4. At 1:30 P.M., the fleet of baby carriages and Axel doppelgängers formed up outside the park and marched into the entertainment area. They gathered onstage in the Pavilion, where each of them received a "valuable and interesting" prize: a Revlon doll for the girls and a "huge" Tonka Fire Truck for the boys. That kicked off the hour-long stage show. The overflow audience was delighted by the onstage shenanigans of WCCO-TV personalities Commodore Cappy, Johnny .44, "Tubby Toby" Prin, Mel Jass, and of course, Axel. Music was provided by the Jimarlen Trio, and a trained dog act added to the fun. At the end of the show, winning tickets were drawn from a barrel and *all* of those fabulous toys were given away.

For two hours afterwards, every ride in the park was free. Gleeful kids could enjoy them as frequently as time and the crowd permitted. With more than 10,000 people in the park, long lines quickly formed at the gate of every attraction, but a free ride was worth a wait. The fun finally came to an end at about five o'clock that afternoon. Another Axel Day was history.

1957 was a pretty good year for Clellan in general. On March 13, he had been awarded a "Minnie" for "Best Children's Show Personality" by the American Federation of Television and Radio Artists and the Advertising Club of Minneapolis for the third year in a row. That October, Axel also climaxed the celebration of Southdale's first anniversary, which began on a Monday with a gigantic seven-foot birthday cake, "a masterpiece of the bakers' art," being offered to shoppers by the millers of Robin Hood Flour. The celebration continued all week, as the mall was host to live radio broadcasts, dixieland jazz concerts, and free pony rides.

The main event took place on Saturday, October 19. Daryl Laub, who by this time had jumped to KSTP-TV and renamed his clown T. N. Tatters, entertained kids in Southdale's Garden Court from 10:00 to 11:00 A.M. Then, from 1:30 till 3:00 P.M., Axel held forth in the same arena. The event drew a tremendous crowd, with kids practically hanging from the balconies. At the end, when a sea of people swarmed around the stage to get the photos that Axel was handing out, it looked as if Elvis had hit town.

The following month, on November 28, Axel was the grand marshal of the St. Paul Thanksgiving Day parade, a spectacular new pageant. One highlight was the first official appearance of twenty-two giant balloons depicting storybook, cartoon, and circus characters (and Santa Claus, of course). An undulating dragon balloon required thirty men to manipulate it as it wound through the streets of the city. The procession also featured the usual floats, bands, marching units, and drum and bugle corps, plus fifteen of the new 1958 convertibles that had been on display at the St. Paul Auto Show in the Auditorium.

Other personalities who joined Axel in the holiday spectacle included Minnesota governor Orville Freeman, St. Paul mayor Joseph Dillon, comic Henny Youngman, violinist Florian Zabach, Miss Minnesota Ardyce Gustafson, King Boreas (James Owens) and Queen of Snows (Eva Wicker) of the Winter Carnival, and Santa Claus himself, in person. Axel was quoted as saying, "I hope there'll be plenty of St. Paul police on duty, 'cause the ladies git so anxious fer my pitcher they try to break trew the police lines!"

The parade began in the Capitol approach at 10:00 A.M., and wound through the Loop for an hour. The whole event was televised by WCCO-TV, with Channel 4 personalities Don O'Brien and John Gallos describing the proceedings for viewers at home. Santa Claus,

  Where do you live, Jack – in the beanstalk?

"who flew in from the North Pole to participate in the parade," was mobbed by children as Gallos attempted to interview him.

Earlier that same fall, Clellan and Marion's sole remaining son, Michael, had moved to Arizona to attend college. For the youngest Card, growing up in Minneapolis had not always been easy. He came of age in the long shadows of his deceased brothers, while his dad's occupation had provided his classmates with a wealth of ammunition for ridicule. "I got a lot of heat in school about my father and his character," he recalled ruefully. "Axel was my nickname in high school, or Towser, or Tallulah. Take your pick." By the time he graduated, Michael was more than ready to leave town and begin a life of his own, in a place where no one had ever heard of Clellan Card or Axel Torgeson.

Once Michael had gone, Clellan and Marion were left alone in the big house on 48th and Colfax. Like many parents faced with an empty nest, they began to consider moving to a smaller place. For years, the Cards had spent their summers at the family cottage in Meadville on Lake Minnetonka. They loved the area, where Clellan was able to indulge his love of boating to the fullest. Ultimately, they decided to move to the lake permanently, buying a Cape Cod-style cottage at 3 MacLynn Road in Excelsior in the spring of 1958.

Their new home sat on a secluded isthmus not far from the old family place in Meadville. The compact yellow house had a flagstone patio surrounded on two sides by a channel that led out to St. Alban's Bay. With three bedrooms and two bathrooms, the cozy domicile had plenty of space. The living room was warmed by a fireplace set at an angle into the wall. The kitchen had all the amenities, even a built-in charcoal grill, so Clellan could charbroil steaks or burgers whenever he liked. Michael described his parents' new home as a "neat little house, brand new. Everything was fresh and clean and newly landscaped – it was a nice place to be, kind of like a little resort. My parents enjoyed it immensely; it was very, very private. I'm glad they did that. They *needed* to do that, desperately. A place that Pete and John had never seen was good for them." Still, leaving the house that had been the family home for nearly twenty years must have been bittersweet.

Another emotionally wrenching event took place at about the same time. On Saturday, April 26, 1958, as he had for the past five years, Clell handled the announcing chores for *Whoopee John's Polka Party*. But this particular evening was different, because it was the program's final broadcast. The date also marked Clellan's last regularly scheduled appearance on radio, the end of a twenty-eight-year run.

Despite his resurgent popularity as a children's television character, Clellan had always considered himself primarily a radio performer. Unfortunately, the medium had changed drastically since the 1930s, but he had not. His routines had remained much the same, and the radio audience had grown tired of them. Even though there was still a considerable reservoir of affection for Clellan among the public, the simple truth was that he no longer could deliver the radio ratings he once had.

WCCO radio's new general manager decided Clellan had to go. Stunned at the news, he asked why he was being dumped. When the manager told him, "Your humor is too old, Clellan," the aging comic shot back, "Is there any *new* humor?" His sarcastic question had a core of truth, but it was no use. He was out.

Mary Davies remembered how devastated Clellan was when WCCO radio dropped him. "He just grieved over that," she said. He really never got over it. During the last years of his life, he made sporadic forlorn attempts to break back into radio, to no avail.

However, Clellan could take some consolation from the fact that, on television, Axel was more popular than ever. In fact, most of WCCO-TV's children's shows were garnering big numbers of small viewers. Channel 4's kidvid drew a larger audience than any other Twin Cities TV station, often larger than all the other stations combined.

In the summer of 1958, WCCO-TV announced the purchase of a "revolutionary" new videotape recording system. A similar one had been used by CBS for three years, but WCCO's was the first such system in the upper Midwest. Videotape offered undeniable benefits: programs could be recorded instantly and played back immediately, or at a later period. And unlike film, videotape could be re-used many times. However, that advantage caused an unfortunate side effect: shooting programs on sixteen-millimeter film soon ceased, since it was faster and easier to videotape a show. However, the tape was expensive so it was used over and over, with each new round

You look like a horse – doctor!

taxonomy (and not to be confused with the earlier Malty Bird), had been added to the program. On this particular morning, the Birdie had an ice pack on its head and was reeling back and forth, obviously hung over. Suddenly, Axel turned to the bird and asked, "Say, Birdie, can I get you a tuna fish malted?"

Another Saturday morning, near the end of the program, Axel said, "Well, kiddies, we've been up here in the tree house for about an hour now, and you've been up for a while, but I'll bet that your parents are still in bed. I think it's about time that they got up, too. So get a glass of water, go into their bedroom, and throw it in their faces, and say, 'Good morning! Time to get up now!'"

After the show, Don turned to Clellan and said, "I don't think you should have done that." Affecting an air of unconcern, Clell brushed off his reproach, saying, "Oh, don't worry about it."

The two of them had just walked into Clellan's office when the telephone rang. For some reason, the star of *Axel and His Dog* was reluctant to answer his own phone, so Don picked it up and intoned, "Clellan Card's office." The woman on the other end of the line snarled, "Put that son of a bitch on!" Don gingerly handed the receiver to Clellan, who answered with great aplomb, "Hellllloooo?" That, however, was the only thing he had a chance to say, as the woman launched into a furious tirade – because, of course, her child had done exactly as Axel had instructed.

Another infamous occasion was the time that Axel told the kids at home about a new game. "Oh, boy, we're going to play games today, ain't we, Towz, hah?" Axel exulted at the beginning of the show. "We've got some extra-special games, y'know – dat 'Duck on the Rock,' dat's a good game. Y'know, I was playin' it one day, and they missed the duck and the rock hit me right on the head. Ha-ha-ha-ha! And I was playing 'Puss in the Corner,' got hit in the puss, laid in the corner for tree hours. I'm tellin' you, dat's a rugged game dere!"

"And we played 'Yerk.' Did you ever play 'Yerk?'" he asked Towser, chuckling. "Dat's one of the more educational type of – " He suddenly whispered conspiratorially to the audience: "You try diss, kids, it's more excitin', see? Now, if you're trew eatin' breakfast, see, all the stuff's settin' on the table," Axel mimed grasping the edge of a table-cloth and continued, "you take a hold of the tablecloth wery firmly in both hands, see? And YERK!" he barked, jerking his hands back, "all of a sudden like dat, and it doesn't even move anyting on the table. Try it some time – you'll find out. Ha-ha-ha-ha!"

When Axel wasn't encouraging kids to create mayhem, he and his pets often would employ double-entendres that slipped past their younger viewers. "Kids could enjoy his humor on one level, and then adults could enjoy it on another level entirely," declared Bob Pratt. "I can remember my mom watching the show and laughing at times, and my brother and I were like, 'What's so funny about that?' Obviously, there was a level of humor there that went right over the heads of kids."

Perhaps the best-remembered running gag on *Axel and His Dog* involved Tallulah's aunt, who lived in the Minneapolis suburb of Anoka. Clellan and Don had great fun talking about her feline abode without ever explicitly using one particular phrase. "Tallulah the cat was always going to visit her aunt's house in Anoka," Don recalled. "If you wanted to perceive it as a cat house, well, there it was – but it was never said in that way."

Tallulah's aunt was a topic of conversation quite often, under all kinds of circumstances. One Sunday, Axel turned to Tallulah and inquired, "Was you at Sunday School today, Tallool?"

"Oh, yeah," affirmed the cat.

"That's good, that's fine," burbled Axel. "How is your Sunday School teacher? Is she that cute one what I seen one day?"

"You know what?" Tallulah interjected. "She's from Anoka."

"Oh, iss she from Anoka?" he said, his interest growing. "Do you s'pose she knows yer aunt over to Anoka?"

"No," Tallulah replied. "I asked her."

"She's never been over to yer aunt's house, hah?" Axel said dubiously. "Well, I suppose there'll be a time when she'll be gettin' over dere."

Tallulah's aunt apparently presided over a real den of iniquity. Not only was it a cat house, it also housed Tallulah's catnip stash. "Oh, Tallool, you look cute this morning," Axel began cheerfully one day. "Say, Towser was over here, you know, a while ago, and he says he has some dognip today. Yessir, and he wondered if you would probably take your dish of catnip and go out with him this afternoon to a movie."

"No, I'm out," Tallulah sniffled. "Out of catnip. I have to go back to Anoka."

the director disbelieve his ears. "We're going to have a aminal guest tomorrow," Axel announced one day. "Tillie is going to be here wisiting tomorrow. Tillie the tassel-twirler! Boy, is she ever a swell kid! Oh, man!"

Her interest piqued, Tallulah asked, "Does she know my aunt?"

"Mmmmm!" groaned Axel. "I was just going on a wery nice subject, when you get nauseratin' again, talking about your aunt over to Anoka. Tillie's going to be here tomorrow. Be sure to be lookin' in, because she's really the funniest girl you ever saw in your life."

Axel said other things that went completely unremarked in his day but which would probably cause a furor now, especially coming from someone who had so much influence on kids. Although Clellan loved women (and the feeling was certainly mutual), he also had a rather condescending view of "the fairer sex." His mindset was typical of his generation – women didn't even have the right to vote until Clell was almost old enough to vote himself. Still, it's hard to overlook the sexism in his occasional offhand remarks portraying women as jealous, greedy creatures who talk too much.

Perhaps most jarring to modern sensibilities was a "ballad" which Axel allegedly wrote, called "I Couldn't Break Her Heart, So I Broke Her Leg." With such a light-hearted allusion to domestic violence, it would doubtless inspire a tidal wave of protest if it were aired on children's television today. At the time, however, no one seems to have even noticed.

For all his freedom to say and do as he pleased on his show, Clellan still chafed at any restrictions on his free-flowing babble. To his mischievous delight, he discovered a way to indulge himself without worrying about the consequences, because viewers knew nothing about it. Filming the Sunday episodes of *Axel and His Dog* had begun in the spring of 1955. To ensure that the film was shown on the correct day, Clellan would announce the airdate at the beginning of the reel. Since those short intros were never intended to be shown publicly, they were a great opportunity for Clell to try to crack up Claude Heisch and WCCO's other film editors.

"Hear this, you louses in the film room!" he bellowed one day. "On this here show, which is December 18th, Sunday, I'm singing a song entitled, 'Mama, Get the Liniment, the Old Man is Stiff Again with Dirty Words.'"

 What did you do when you saw the home – run?

Clellan and Don had both built their careers working live: on stage, on radio, and on television. They knew all too well that on a live show, a mistake could not be corrected; performers just had to carry on as best they could. So the two seasoned pros were quick to appreciate the benefits of pre-recording programs. Filming gave them a luxury they had rarely had before: the possibility of retakes. It wasn't long before they realized that it also meant that they could have a lot of fun. Once a take was blown, Clell and Don could (and did) take all sorts of liberties with the material, much to the crew's amusement. However, these out-takes, funny as they might be, remained a private joke among the employees of WCCO-TV. The public never saw them, because the expletives and ribald humor would have shattered Axel's image.

During filming, when Clellan tripped over his own tongue or made some other mistake, he might unleash some mild profanity (which, of course, he would never do during live broadcasts). "Hi, kids! Diss is Axel!" he began as usual one day. "Happy Sunday to you, and I hope you have the walls – the wahs – wahs – [*whistle*] Double stink, poop, and fart!" He made a face as the crew giggled off-camera.

One day when he fouled up, Axel hilariously broke character and metamorphosed into a demented old curmudgeon. He was trying to promote a contest for local sponsor the Trading Post–Skate Exchange – and he'd already stumbled over the message at least once. "Now, next Friday, I'm going to announce ten winners of these cute Pinocchio dolls," he started again, holding up one hand with his fingers outstretched, "ten of 'em, five times two, and you might be one of the winners. You know, when you write in for the contest, whether you win one of these cute Pinocchio dolls or not, I'm going to send you a skating book, lesson folder, or – " Axel stared blankly for a moment as his memory failed him, " – a goddamn book, ha-ha-ha!"

Knowing that another take was ruined, Axel suddenly growled at the camera, "Get the letters in or I'll kick your little red asses, you little buggers!" Laughter erupted from the stagehands as Axel grabbed the placard plastered with the sponsor's name and address. "And don't go over here, they're lousy, see! Goddamn, I ain't going over dere myself! Ha-ha-ha-ha-hmmmm!" He grimaced malevolently and shoved his face up against the doll's, bringing the spot to a suitably deranged finish.

  Say, do you have a pen – pal?

Occasionally, the cast and crew staged bits for their own amusement. Once, Clellan and Don had some fun at the expense of fellow kidvid host Johnny .44, played by Jack Hastings. The camera zoomed in on the Malty Bird, perched in his nest as usual, except a cigarette dangled from his bill, the smoke curling around his small, bulbous head. Axel, stretching and blinking his eyes sleepily, walked in and said with a yawn, "Oh, boy! How long before that Johnny .44'll be through, that peckerwood – ain't he a loudmouth old fart?"

"He's a shithead," Malty agreed, in his weird high-pitched squeak.

"Shithead .44, you mean?" Axel laughed. "That's the name for him, eh? Malty, you got it. Hit it right in the head, dere."

One Christmas season, WCCO-TV filmed short holiday greetings, to be aired during station breaks, from each of their leading personalities. Axel was included, of course, but in addition to the regular message, he also did another rendition, probably to amuse the WCCO-TV employees at the station's own Christmas party. Axel's face appeared on-screen, framed by a festive Christmas wreath. "Hi, all you peckerwoods out there!" he hollered drunkenly, swaying from side to side. "I hope you don't get stinkin' from your drinkin' this holiday season! Ha-ha-ha-HIC!" With that, his eyes rolled back in his head, and he slowly slid down out of sight.

Clellan gave another pickled performance during the infamous sloshed excursion on Lake Minnetonka, a.k.a. the Foojeerian Sea. Wearing a stylish nautical cap, Axel sat near the ribbed steering wheel at the stern of the watercraft, clutching a bottle of Scotch. Waves rippled across the surface of the water behind him. "Oohh, over the bounding sea!" he sang woozily, gulped a slug of booze, then upended the bottle and sprinkled some on his head. "Oh, say! I ran across some of them foo birds," he announced in a loud voice. "You know, if you don't shoot 'em on the first time, if you just wing 'em, they crap right over ya and pin ya right to the ground, ya know. And there's a old legend that if you wash that crap offa ya, why, you'll drop dead! Ha-ha-ha! Ooohh!"

Axel took another hefty swig from his bottle. "Hic! Uhhh, I – I shot at one of them foo birds and I winged him, see, I didn't kill him, and he crapped all over me. And I sess, 'Wash the crap offa me! I don't give a goddamn whether they have any legends or not!' And you know what happened to me? I dropped dead right on the spot!

And from that, they have the old familiar saying: 'If the foo shits, wear it!'"

Which only goes to show that even Clellan's *dirty* jokes were excruciating puns.

Besides scatological out-takes, something else about *Axel and His Dog* escaped even the most discerning viewers. Around April of 1959, Bill Dietrichson created a new Tree House set. As a sort of private joke, he painted the whole thing, from the familiar tree trunk to a fanciful cuckoo clock, in a hallucinatory blue, with pink highlights. Since the show was seen only in black and white, no one outside the station was the wiser. The bizarrely colored *mise en scène* turned out to be the most enduring tree house set of all, lasting until the end of 1964.

Meanwhile, other things in Axel's Tree House seemed to swell in size. His spyglass grew to four feet or more, with his name lettered on the side – but it still looked as wonderfully cheesy as ever. At some point, Axel also procured a gigantic three-foot comb for his "How do my curls look?" bit, straightening his hair with its gargantuan teeth. Since the comb was large enough to be visible at a distance, it also proved to be a good prop to brandish at events such as the Aquatennial parade.

In the late 1950s, Axel's popularity continued unabated, as his ratings graphically demonstrate. He nearly always won his time slot, and often by phenominal margins. On Mondays in January 1959, for example, his rating was over 20, while his nearest competitor had less than 7 – none other than *American Bandstand*, Dick Clark's network show. Axel's numbers did fluctuate – for one thing, they declined every year as spring gave way to summer and kids spent more time playing outside than watching TV inside – but he remained a ratings powerhouse as the 1960s dawned.

His personal appearances were still going great guns as well. Another Axel Day was held in Excelsior Amusement Park on June 20, 1959. As things turned out it was the final one, although they weren't discontinued due to declining interest. Twelve thousand kids showed up that year to see Axel, Carmen, Rocko Dyne (Jack Hastings), Captain Dale (Dale Woodley), and Bud Kraehling as the "Foremost Foreman." The problem was that the lion's share of the crowds came from the Lake Minnetonka area, as the entries in the various

What kind of gas do you use – Ethel?

Axel doing his TV show in front of a fascinated crowd at the 1960 Minnesota State Fair

Axel Day contests had revealed. Channel 4 had hoped to reach a wider cross section of the population with their celebration, so the plug was pulled on the rather expensive promotion.

It was thought that the Minnesota State Fair would be a more effective way to make contact with people from all across the state. WCCO-TV acquired a large space in the Grandstand, with plans to broadcast a number of programs live from the 1960 State Fair. Among other things, this would give audiences a rare opportunity to see Axel doing his show in person. He didn't disappoint them, carrying on with special guests, reading viewers' letters, announcing contests, pushing products, and handing out Axel trading cards by the fistful. Towser and Tallulah made one awkward appearance at the fair but aside from that, they stayed back in the tree house.

The State Fair venture was a tremendous success for WCCO-TV, drawing huge crowds eager to see their favorite shows in action. The idea was such a hit that the station maintains a strong presence at the Minnesota State Fair to this day.

However, the end of Axel Day didn't mean that the nutty Norseman abandoned Excelsior Amusement Park – far from it. In the early 1960s, he celebrated his "birthday" there, often with a stage show much like those featured during Axel Days. At the end of the school

Axel on the set at the 1960 Minnesota State Fair

year, he also made trips to the park to give good students free tickets to ride. Each child who brought his or her report card received four ride tickets for every A and two ride tickets for every B in academic subjects.

On Sunday, May 29, 1960, a mammoth display of fireworks commemorated Memorial Day and the full-time opening of Excelsior Amusement Park for its thirty-fifth season. Two attractions made their debut that year. One was a hot rods ride, imported from Germany, featuring five-horsepower cars that raced around an oval wooden track. The other was Axel's Laff House.

Previously the House of Mystery attraction, Axel's Laff House was a fairly typical fun house, where guests had to negotiate their way through a large rotating cylinder, among other obstacles. The main draw was a labyrinth of looking glasses. Hundreds of full-length mirrors, reflecting images into infinity, created a baffling maze for anyone attempting to negotiate a way through it. Here and there, the array of reflectors was spiked with a distorting mirror that twisted the images into weird shapes. Outside, suspended above the entrance in a glass booth, Axel's Laff House boasted a life-size animated model of Axel, complete with spyglass, his head bobbing back and forth, "inwiting" guests inside with a special recording of the old Scandihoovian's voice, over a chorus of raucous laughter.

In 1961, Axel made an effort to upgrade his image. He abandoned his crude cardboard spyglass, and acquired what appeared to be a real, honest-to-goodness telescope. That fall, he made the first major alteration in his costume since perfecting his look in 1954. A large capital *A* in sequins, surrounded by a spangled border, was added to the brim of his engineer's cap. It may have been about this time that

MY MOST EMBARASSING MOMENT

My wife met me at the television studio one afternoon before Christmas so we could do the remainder of our errands together, which are always multifold at that time of year. As we were going down in the elevator, it stopped, and an extremely shapely red-head got on the elevator. She poked me in the ribs and said – "Hi, Sweetie Pie."

My wife didn't bat an eyelash, she just smiled, and said – "I'm Mrs. Pie!"

Every once in a while in his column, Clell offered an evocative reminiscence of his youth, or an actual opinion about one of the burning issues of the day:

The Minnesota Twins baseball team deserves plenty of praise from all of us in this new major league area. Too many people are too ready and willing to criticize. Have you ever noticed that these loud mouth gripers are generally the people that don't have too much to do anyway – so whats left to do but gripe!

When a sophomore year trans-plant, like the Twins, can step along one-two-three with teams that have been established for years and years and have plenty of dough to pick the cream of the crop – we're completely nuts if we do anything but support the Twins to the hilt. Man what a world series would do for the Twin Cities.

Despite signs that he was becoming a more accomplished writer, though, Clellan's column didn't outlast the summer. The final installment appeared on August 23.

The alliance between Axel and Rocky was equally short-lived. In September, the flying squirrel took off and Axel teamed with an even more unlikely partner: Bomba the Jungle Boy. Shown in theaters from 1949 to 1955, the *Bomba* films were a series of low-budget adventure flicks based on a popular character of juvenile fiction, a sort of Tarzan Junior. In fact, Bomba was played by Johnny Sheffield, who first wore a loincloth as Boy in the *Tarzan* series. The *Bomba* movies lacked big-budget production values, but they did have a certain schlocky kid appeal.

Running *Bomba* on Axel's show seems to have been a last-minute decision. Shortly before the jungle series began, it was announced that Bomba would *replace* Axel. That such a radical course of action was even considered is an indication of the disarray left in the wake of Don's departure from the program. As things turned out, Axel stayed on to host the *Bomba* series, but the tree house dweller and the Jungle Boy were not a good match – the two characters simply had no affinity for each other, unlike Axel and the Little Rascals. Besides, the longer *Bomba* films had to be awkwardly edited to fit into the time slot. Worst of all, Bomba got his butt kicked by Mickey Mouse in the all-important ratings race. For example, during November 1962, Axel averaged 63,200 viewers, while the Mouse garnered 75,000. After only three months, Bomba was abandoned.

In mid-December, Axel began showing a film series that was more in line with his refined sensibilities: *The Bowery Boys*. Although not in the same league as the Hal Roach comedies, the *Bowery Boys* films managed to be amusing often enough, thanks primarily to Leo Gorcey and Huntz Hall, who starred as malaprop-prone Slip Mahoney and the moronic but stupid Sach Jones, respectively. What the Bowery Boys lacked in sophistication, they more than made up for in raw numbers. Within weeks, Axel's viewer totals skyrocketed to 92,800 for the month of January 1963, this time clobbering Mickey, who had a mere 80,900.

Elsewhere at "Canal 4," kiddie host John Gallos had also undergone some changes. After two years as Commodore Cappy, and two years as Clancy the [Keystone] Cop, who had a voice that owed a lot to Bob Hope's mustachioed sidekick Jerry Colonna ("Aaaaahhh, yes!"), in the fall of 1961 he had metamorphosed into the futuristic Clancy the Space Cop, in a vain effort to exploit the space race. After one season the Space Cop vaporized, leaving Axel to carry the brunt of WCCO-TV's afternoon kiddie schedule for some time. But then on Tuesday, September 3, 1963, Clancy the Cop returned as a modern-day character. Unlike his predecessors, this contemporary policeman was not so much a characterization as he was a reflection of the real John Gallos. This version of Clancy also proved to be Gallos's most enduring role, appearing on Channel 4 for more than thirteen years.

The new show, set in a small detective agency, was initially called *Clancy and Company*. The "and Company" part was provided by aspiring theater actor Allan Lotsberg. "John needed somebody to talk to," Allan says, "because we found out that teams work a lot better than somebody talking into a lens – and if you've ever done that, it gets real lonesome out there."

Allan had gotten his start in WCCO-TV's promotion department in

August 1961, writing promo spots and the like. Harry Jones recruited him one day to handle a witch puppet named Vivian Vulture on the new children's show. The young neophyte managed to avoid causing any major disasters during the program, so Harry asked him if he would be willing to appear on-screen. At first, Allan demurred – he was a serious actor, after all – but after a week or so, Harry persuaded him to rent a costume and give it a try. On the program the next day, Clancy walked over to the portrait of Sherlock Groans, the founder of the detective agency, and tweaked his nose. The picture slid up, a big door opened, and then a wheeled box came rolling onto the set, carrying a silly little guy dressed in a hound's-tooth checked suit, his legs akimbo. "Ah! It's Willie Ketchem!" Clancy exclaimed.

Willie quickly became an integral part of the show, his youthful, bumbling exuberance balancing Clancy's reserved and somewhat obtuse persona. Later, Allan developed other characters for the show in addition to Vivian Vulture, notably Willie's Auntie Ketchem, who persistently called her nephew's superior "Clanky," and Wilfred the Wiener Wolf, a furry puppet with a predilection for a particular sponsor's products.

Unlike *Axel and His Dog*, Clancy's show also had actual storylines. Often centering around a trivial mystery or a lighthearted adventure, a yarn might be told in one self-contained episode or strung out over several weeks, depending on the strength of the material and the needs of the moment. Allan and Harry usually developed the rough plot, which John and Allan would improvise around from day to day until the tale reached its resolution. Another memorable aspect of *Clancy and Company* was its rousing theme song: an excerpt from "Dance of the Hours" as performed by Spike Jones and His City Slickers, complete with gun shots.

About the time that *Clancy and Company* was launched, or possibly a bit earlier, Axel's show was revamped. It got nutty new theme music, along the lines of Clancy's kooky Spike Jones song. Axel's tune, though performed by a more obscure group of musicians, was no less inspired: "The Lonesome Road" by Dean Elliot and His Swinging Big, Big Band. In its complete form, "The Lonesome Road" is a two-and-a-half-minute aural opus dramatizing one of the classic themes of literature: boy gets car, boy meets girl, boy gets fresh and loses girl.

What did you have for dinner, baby – beets?

Of course, only a short piece of the song was used for Axel's theme, but what really distinguished "The Lonesome Road" was its inventive use of sound effects. The nearly wordless story unfolds when an old jalopy coughs into life, and the auto's rhythmic wheezes and knocks punctuate the melody. Dean Elliot scored each sound effect, writing parts for them as if they were standard musical instruments. The result was wonderfully goofy, and perfect for Axel.

The other major problem with the program was also finally solved. Just as John Gallos needed a partner to talk to, so did Clellan – and one was close at hand. Ever since she had been enlisted as Carmen the Nurse back in October 1954, Mary Davies had continued to serve as the show's substitute host whenever Clellan couldn't be there. She also made sporadic appearances with Axel on the program from time to time. But Carmen Kissleman (her last name bequeathed by Clellan) began making daily trips to Axel's Tree House when Mary Davies became the regular co-host of the show, probably in early 1963.[24]

In some ways, things didn't change much. The stagehands still gleefully concocted on-air surprises for Clellan from product samples awaiting the day's commercials. They mixed chalk and water to replace milk, or used the radiator to sour cartons of chocolate milk and to turn Twinkies rock-hard so Axel couldn't break them open to show the creamy filling. At such moments, his expressions were "priceless," Mary recalled with a laugh. "You can look at just so many Twinkies and Ho-Hos before something has to be done!"

In other ways, though, the show's atmosphere was quite different from what it had been. As Clellan aged, Axel began to seem more like a nutty old uncle than an overgrown kid. More significantly, Carmen ushered in a kinder, gentler program, one that seemed geared more to younger children than the original show. Viewers heard fewer arguments, fewer references to catnip, and fewer "ain'ts" – and more public service messages, more references to school, and more "don'ts." The program lost much of its acerbic edge.

Some longtime fans of the show felt that Mary didn't click with Clellan as well as Don had. Where Axel was wacky, boisterous, and unpredictable, Carmen could seem cloying, condescending, and didactic. The difference between the two was epitomized in the way that they referred to the off-screen members of the stage crew. Axel called them "the skunks in the forest." In Carmen's mouth, that pungent epithet was corrupted into the more infantile term "skunkies."

Mary herself was somewhat mystified about why Clell chose to have her on the air with him. Her best guess: because she laughed at his jokes. "I was there much more as an audience than as a co-worker," she admitted. She had idolized Clellan ever since she first heard him on the radio. When she began working with him on television, she was still a little bit in awe of him and constantly surprised by what came out of his mouth. When Axel made a wisecrack, instead of coming up with a snappy retort the way Tallulah would, Carmen was often reduced to helpless laughter. A case in point occurred on a show broadcast near the end of one December.

"Say, some of the udder things you got for Christmas," Axel suddenly said to Carmen, "you got a spray for those fruit flies that fly around your head, didn't ya?"

"Yes," Carmen replied, and began to giggle uncontrollably.

"Isn't that nice?" Axel murmured. "Isn't that cute? That's helpful, I think."

Carmen gasped between bursts of laughter, "– Grandma Torgeson –"

"I hope you use it before you come in here," interrupted Axel. "Did Grandma Torgeson let you use her slingshot?"

Axel and Carmen

Carmen managed to say, "– She gave me the fru – fruit fly spray –" before dissolving into a gale of guffaws.

"You're having one of your attacks, aren't you, Carmine?" Axel chuckled. "Your en-yin is running. Well, you better pewt it in neutral and rest awhile."

When she wasn't convulsed with laughter by Axel's remarks, Carmen sometimes could do little more than gape at him. One morning, she arrived at the tree house after paying a visit to Grandma Torgeson at "the home."

"Well, how is Grandma?" wondered Axel.

"Oh, she's fine," Carmen responded. "All the ladies are just fine. They said to say hello to you and the kids. Hi, kids."

"How are Grandma's warts?" Axel abruptly asked.

There was silence for a moment. "Well, uh – " stammered Carmen.

"She's been upset by warts all her life, y'know," he explained.

Carmen countered weakly, "Well, she's not complaining."

"That little wart she married, she wasn't too happy wit', y'know," Axel declared. "Speaking of warts, y'know, Grandpa Torgeson had a wart right on the back of his neck. He used it for a collar button all the time. Ha-ha-ha-ha-ha!"

Better suited to the role of straight man, Mary had difficulty telling a joke even when Clellan coached her. One day before they went on the air, he said to her, "I'm going to let you be funny today. Now, I'll ask you a question, and you say, 'Dog hair.'" She nodded, and began repeating her line of dialogue over and over to herself in an effort to memorize it.

During the show, Axel turned to Carmen and asked, "What do you call the last hair on a dog's tail?"

She looked at him and replied, "The last hair." Axel cracked up, but no one else could figure out why it was so funny.[25]

On the other hand, many people found Carmen's warm-hearted manner appealing. She brought a maternal softness to the proceedings that toddlers in particular found comforting. Her infectious laugh often prompted laughter from the audience as well. In her starched white nurse's uniform, she even had a certain sex appeal; more than one adolescent boy had a crush on her.

And Carmen did strike a note of kooky humor once in a while.

  What would you do if she stole your clothes – hanger?

There was the time she was making oatmeal cookies and Axel asked for one. She handed him a cookie, and a moment later, he hesitantly inquired, "Aren't dese oatmeal cookies a little soggy?"

"They're supposed to be," Carmen answered, "I haven't baked them yet."

When Tonka Toys became a sponsor, their sturdy vehicles were regularly given away to kids who wrote in. One day, just before drawing the winning postcard, Axel was extolling the virtues of the "classy" Tonka trucks at length when Carmen added, "The wheels are round, too."

For Christmas one year, she gave Axel a "different" sort of present. "Oh! Isn't that nice!" Axel exclaimed when he tore off the wrapping paper. "That's the prettiest I've ever seen!" he raved, then abruptly asked, "What is it?"

"Well, it's – it's a board," Carmen said.

"A board?" Axel repeated quizzically. "Yeah, I guess I get the idea."

"Well, you know, for the roof," prompted Carmen. "You've been wanting to fix the roof; well, there's the board. Now you can fix it."

Suddenly it dawned on him. "Oh, the roof! Yeah, the leak in the roof – it's just what I wanted."

Axel admired his present for a moment, and sniffed the fragrant aroma of the wood. "You shouldn't have done it, Carmine," he protested. "To spend your good money on something nice like diss." Then he turned and muttered to the audience, "I think she swiped it out of a lumberyard."

But without Don, what about Towser and Tallulah? He had been their voices and personalities for eight years – Don *was* that dog and that cat. The two pets were too much a part of the show to simply be eliminated, so Mary was suddenly thrust into those long, long gloves and had to do the best she could. It was as if Robert Goulet had been recruited to replace Shari Lewis as Lamb Chop.

Harry Jones didn't think that Mary could do Towser's gruff, wordless voice at all, so the poor dog was hardly ever heard from again. Axel wouldn't abandon his loyal pooch entirely, though, so he still talked about Towser occasionally. Eventually, the dog was exiled to the tree house projection booth, so whenever it was time to show a *Deputy Dawg* cartoon or a *Little Rascals* episode (yes, they came back yet again), Axel would exhort his mute mutt to "Pewt on the movie, Towz!"

The neurotic, hyperactive Tallulah couldn't be disposed of as easily as the inarticulate Towser. She had become known for talking back to Axel, and her gadfly role had given her more prominence. She couldn't just fade into the woodwork. Mary was able to muster a passable imitation of Tallulah, so she began playing the cat in addition to Carmen.

The two female characters had a rivalry that went way back. In 1956, when Axel sailed off across the Foojeerian Sea on his "yatch," he left Carmen in charge of the tree house. He returned to find a tearful Tallulah whining because the young nurse had paid too much attention to Towser. She complained to Axel that Carmen had "exhibited favoritism." "She *has?*" Axel gasped, clearly shocked. "That's one thing I told Carmine *never* to exhibit."

Carmen and Tallulah's mutual dislike simplified things, because it suggested a reason why the two were almost never seen together. The real explanation, of course, was that Mary couldn't play both characters simultaneously. Because her impersonation of Tallulah left something to be desired – at least as far as Harry was concerned – as time went on, the peevish feline was heard from less and less, although she never disappeared completely.

When Mary became pregnant in 1963, it was decided to keep her off-screen once her pregnancy started to show rather than raise all sorts of messy questions in young viewers' minds. Harry also wanted her to avoid playing Tallulah as much as possible, so a new cat character was created: FiFi La Tour. In contrast to Tallulah's comparatively plain appearance, FiFi's paw was boldly tiger-striped, accented with bright nail polish and a bracelet.

FiFi's personality also stood in contrast to Tallulah's. Where Don's cat was whiny and argumentative, the new feline was "just as sweet as Carmen." Mary calls FiFi "quite an elegant girl. She was sort of my entertainer side. I think she was Carmen's flip side." FiFi was allegedly Tallulah's cousin, but if her mother was the notorious aunt from Anoka, she doesn't seem to have mentioned it.

By this time, the show's off-the-wall humor may have ebbed somewhat, but that might not have been due solely to Carmen's relatively decorous presence. Clellan was nearing sixty and slowing

I hear you're nuts about the navy-bean!

CHAPTER **19**

PRESiDENT AXEL

ON THE VERY LAST DAY OF 1964, Carmen was busy packing. No, she wasn't leaving Axel; the two of them were moving to a new tree house, and a new time slot. She talked to herself as she packed and stacked stuff near the door. "If I've said it once, I've said it a hundred times: if you want something done, do it yourself. He keeps saying, 'Well, wait for the van, wait for the van.' Well, in the meantime, a person just has to get packed!" Breathing heavily from her exertions, she went on, "But we haven't gotten any packing done here for the big move to seven o'clock next Monday, and now this just leaves a few hours, and I don't see Axel. I suppose he's down in the forest, visiting with Mr. Johnson [the proprietor of the general store on Magic Island] or something."

The moving van was late, so Carmen called Willie Ketchem and asked him to find out why it hadn't arrived yet. No sooner had she hung up the receiver when Axel finally showed up, laughing and joking. She told him about her conversation with the young detective but then Axel said accusingly, "You are just trying to make me jealous by saying you were talkin' to Ketchem."

Carmen explained that she only called Willie to find out what happened to the moving van. "I'm having Clancy follow you and Ketchem," Axel declared, "because you got sumpin' goin' with Ketchem."

The nurse brushed off his suspicions. "Oh, never you mind," she demurred. "It's just a great admiration."

Later in the program, Axel revealed that the movers "had an extra-heavy schedule, they said they had to make some extra stops, so the movin' van isn't gettin' here till tomorrow night."

This came as news to Carmen. "But Willie did check out – "

"Yah, he checked out quick when he found out I didn't like the fact that he was messin' around, and hangin' around you all da time," the jealous hermit muttered darkly.

Carmen tried to lighten the mood. "Well, he doesn't really hang around, Axel, he just *advises* me on things."

"Yah, I was advisin' him on a few tings, too," replied Axel, his voice laced with sarcasm. "I advised him not to hang around the tree house too much."

"Well, he just does it in a sleuthing vein," Carmen protested.

"Yes, he was inwestigatin', he says," the old Scandihoovian snorted. "Yah, sits up in that tree over dere, lookin' in the windows here alla time."

Axel couldn't stay mad at Carmen, though; by the time they signed off, they were trading silly "old Shakespeneerian sayings." Aside from the undertones of jealousy and even voyeurism in that particular episode, however, there was more going on beneath the show's surface than viewers could have guessed. A number of changes were in the offing.

After more than five years of use, the backdrop featuring the cuckoo clock was a cracked and peeling eyesore. In terrible condition, it had to be replaced. The necessity of redoing the set was camouflaged with the pretext of the big move, which also encompassed the impending switch to a morning time slot. Since 1962, Axel had been appearing in his short segment on the *Siegfried, the Flying Saucer* morning show, but beginning January 4, 1965, a half-hour in the early morning would be his sole venue. Why, after more than ten years as the lord of the afternoon, was Axel banished to the dawn hours?

Carmen and Grandma Torgeson

Although his lead in the

How do you like your eggs, Sigmund – Freud?

ratings may not have been as commanding as it once was, he still usually won his time period. In February 1964, for example, he garnered a rating of 9, while his competition on WTCN had 8, KSTP 7, and KMSP 4. That same month, the afternoon edition of *Axel* reached 63,250 homes, while the morning version was seen in only 36,600. The early show did demonstrate steady growth in viewership over the first four months of 1964, but the after-school program still pulled a larger audience. So why remove Axel from his traditional afternoon period, where he was usually top-rated and could draw nearly twice as many viewers as he could in the morning?

Ironically, part of the answer lies in those same viewership numbers. Advertisers naturally wanted to reach the largest possible audience, which made afternoons more desirable than mornings. They also preferred to make their pitches to adults, who had more disposable income than children did. The stations, meanwhile, wanted to attract an adult audience in the afternoon in order to give their all-important news programs a strong lead-in. They also discovered that programming for adults in those time periods produced more revenue than the kid shows ever could, so it didn't really matter how large the audience was for the kids' shows.

"The key word here is 'demographics,'" explained Sonny Fox, former NBC children's television vice president. "When local stations got more sophisticated about demographics, they found out that in the after-school slots, although they could sell kids' shows, the bucks they could get for the minute didn't begin to compare to the money they would earn if they sold to a women's audience."

And so, as children's programming around the country was moved to less-desirable time periods, *Axel* was shuffled off to 7:00 A.M. Clellan may not have minded, anyway. After all, *Almanac of the Air*, his first real success so many years ago, had aired at seven o'clock, too. Besides, by the 1960s videotape made it possible to prerecord the show at any time, so he didn't actually have to go down to the studio early in the morning anymore.

By the time that the tree house set was renovated for the new morning show, designer Bill Dietrichson was no longer at the station, so the new set was constructed by other hands. The result was pleasant enough, but lacked the spark of Dietrichson's best creations. A low paneled wall stretched the length of the tree house, interrupted at intervals by tall posts supporting the shingled eaves of the roof. A few awkward branches splayed across the background. A gingerbread door on the right served as the new entrance. In the foreground, the crotch of the tree was repainted for only the third time since 1955.

When Axel and Carmen moved in to their new digs, a number of other innovations on *Axel* were already well established. His costume had evolved yet again. The sequins on his engineer's cap, first appearing in the fall of 1961, had spread along his shoulders and across his stomach two years later. By 1964, gold spangles crisscrossed his cap from front to back, and a double row of the shiny dots encircled his collar and ran the length of his shirt sleeves. At the same time, he finally abandoned his suspenders, entrusting his pale blue pants to his triple-strength rope belt alone. This alteration may have been prompted by a desire to accommodate a crowd of colorful medals. Starting with a single police badge in 1963, his chest gradually became encrusted with decorations made by youngters especially for their hero. It was the sort of thing that perpetuated itself: at first, one or two kids sent him their homemade medals. As soon as Axel wore them, other children jumped on the bandwagon. Before long, chest emblems were arriving in the mail on a regular basis.

Axel in 1964

In keeping with his early morning hours, and harking all the way back to *Almanac of the Air*, Axel had developed some running gags about drinking coffee. Whenever he poured himself a cup, the gurgling liquid flowed out of the pot for an absurdly long time. "Just a mouthful," he would say as he topped off his mug, after pouring what sounded like gallons of coffee. Then, when he took a swig, the java's passage down his gullet was heralded by a descending slide whistle, followed by a resounding splat when the gulp reached its destination.

In fact, by this time, the percolator with the fly-away lid had become a Magic Coffeepot. It did more than simply provide liquid refreshment: when the lid was raised, it could also play music. Sometimes a few bars of a tune would accidently blare at inopportune moments, but Axel and Carmen also took advantage of the coffeepot's musical properties to dance around the tree house when the mood struck them. The Magic Coffeepot had grown out of one of Mary's ideas. She originally suggested a Magic Piano to give her an opportunity to do some singing on the show. "Never came about," she complained. "If I wanted something that cost over five cents, there was no question about it, I wasn't going to get it. They were no-budget shows – they were absolutely the no-est-budget shows that were ever produced."

Besides coffee, Axel had another favorite beverage by this time: a mysterious concoction known as Hector's Nectar. The properties of this fabled elixir aren't known in detail, although one quality was beyond doubt: Axel often proclaimed that it was "boneless." Hector's Nectar seems to have been quite a bracing brew. Mary felt that it was Clellan's code for an alcoholic beverage.

In the summer of 1964, two teenage girls became smitten with the show, setting in motion a chain of events that would shape the last era of *Axel*. Like most Twin Cities kids, they'd watched the program when they were younger but hadn't seen it since Carmen had become Axel's sidekick. The pair of high school students, Julie Moden and Carol Schaubach, were quite taken with the way the two co-stars joked back and forth. It may seem surprising that fifteen-year-olds would be interested in a children's television show, but while it's true that the girls were older than most of *Axel*'s audience, they were hardly alone. Adults had always comprised a significant portion of the old Scandihoovian's viewership, registering as high as 48 percent in January 1956 but more typically ranging from 10 to 20 percent of the total.

Charged with enthusiasm for their new idols, Julie and Carol began hanging around the Channel 4 studios. They met their TV favorites briefly the first time they visited the station in September 1964. After that, they became even more infatuated with the program and began to watch tapings of *Axel* surreptitiously from the street, peering through a gap in the curtains drawn across the "Weather Window." One afternoon, Julie and Carol saw Mary put on Tallulah's paw to play the cat. "You've never seen such funny expressions on someone's face!" Julie wrote later in her "History of the Axel and Carmen Fan Club." "At the end of the show, Tallulah threw a pie in Axel's face! You should have seen how hard Carmen was laughing then!! I bet she really enjoyed doing that!! Axel walked by the window with his face covered with pie. He was laughing too."

Another time, they saw Clellan as he was leaving the television station. Their hero smiled cheerfully at them. "He looked so handsome and dignified," Julie noted. "He really looked like a celebrity that just stepped out of a men's fashion magazine! If he only knew how often we stood outside WCCO hoping to see him come through those doors."

Casting about for a legitimate reason to get inside the station, Julie hit on the idea of preparing a school speech about how a television camera works. The two teens returned to the WCCO-TV building, but lost their nerve and instead stood around outside, feverishly debating what to say. Screwing up their courage, they finally marched through the big glass doors into the lobby. Julie explained to the receptionist why they were there, and she called someone on the switchboard. While they were waiting, Clellan passed through the lobby, "dressed in his regular clothes and looking kind of serious." Shortly after, the receptionist told them to go up to the Promotion Department office. There Tom Cousins, the head of the department, gave them the information about TV cameras that they wanted. They sat and talked in his office for a while.

Afterward, the two girls decided that they needed an idea that would enable them to spend time at WCCO-TV "without just standing around like a couple of idiots." Since Axel was such an idol to kids, they decided that the perfect solution would be to start a fan club. They wrote a letter to Cousins, outlining their proposal. Julie drew up a sample membership card and button, including them with the letter. After what seemed like forever, an answer came in mid-December 1964. Tom Cousins wrote that he was "intrigued by the idea" of a fan club and wanted to discuss it further. After the two

Carmen watches Axel mull things over

girls stopped screaming with excitement, Carol called the station and made an appointment for them to meet with Mr. Cousins just after Christmas. That day he took them on a tour of the station, showing them the station's own print shop where copies of the fan club's newsletter would be printed. They made arrangements to meet again in a month, when the girls promised to have the first issue of the newsletter ready.

The inaugural issue of the *Tree House Tribune* contained the first installments of several regular features: "Bobo Reports," the latest headlines from Magic Island reported by a character called Bobo Bunny; "Grandma Torgeson's Column," containing "a proverb or two and some good, sound advice" from the tree house's venerable old matriarch; "Life with Axel," a crudely-drawn cartoon chronicling Axel's antics; and "Dear Stinky," a question-and-answer feature allegedly written by one of the skunks of the forest. That first newsletter also had jokes, riddles, a crossword puzzle, a drawing to color, and a column called "Dates to Remember" – which in the first issue was completely blank! Despite (or perhaps because of) the *Tree House*

May I hold your hand – *bag?*

Tribune's amateurish quality, Cousins decided that he liked it well enough to authorize printing 1,000 copies.

Julie and Carol came back downtown on February 1, 1965, for their first "official meeting," which turned out to be lunch at the Sheraton Ritz. To their amazement, they dined with Clellan, Mary, Harry, and Tom Cousins. Having lunch with "all these important people" made both girls nervous, but Mary went out of her way to make them feel comfortable while Clellan amused them with his funny remarks and stories of the old days in radio and television. "Boy, he's really been around!" Julie wrote in admiration. The group discussed the fan club idea, and the two teens could hardly believe their ears when it was decided that both of them should appear on the *Axel* show to announce the founding of "The Axel and Carmen Fan Club."

Julie described her impressions of their arrival at WCCO-TV for their television premiere on Monday, March 1, 1965:

> *The big day is finally here! Our TV debut! We could hardly get through the school day because we were so excited! We got to the station at 4:00 & the receptionist told Tom Cousins we were there. I was so nervous I was almost sick to my stomach. What if I threw up!*
>
> *After he explained what would happen, he took us up to Studio 4. We went through a big heavy door into a huge studio. It was kind of dark in there except for the lights shining on the Axel set. There was a counter like what could have been used for a news show directly to our left. Then the Axel set was next to that. Across the far back wall was the set for the Clancy show.*
>
> *There were quite a few cameras & lots of big cables on the floor. We had to watch where we were stepping. There were a lot of big lights hanging down from the very high ceiling and we could see some dim lights up in the control room. We could hear Harry Jones calling down directions from up there.*
>
> *Axel wasn't going to be on the show that day. I don't know where he was but it would have been fun if he had been there. As the time got closer for us to go on I felt like I could die! Tom Cousins said, "Now girls, don't get the giggles." I was way too nervous to get the giggles!*

In that day's episode of *Axel*, Carmen got a telegram from "Two Mysterious Strangers" saying that they would be arriving in the tree house soon with "wonderful exciting news." This sent Carmen into a dither until finally Julie and Carol marched in, carrying signs urging kids to send 25 cents to WCCO-TV. After introducing themselves in nearly inaudible voices, the girls hesitantly described the Axel and Carmen Fan Club. For a quarter, kids would get a membership card, an Axel Safety Sticker, a picture of Axel and Carmen, and a subscription to the *Tree House Tribune*.

The coins poured in. Eventually, the Axel and Carmen Fan Club grew to more than 1,400 members. The two presidents devoted a lot of time and effort to their expanding club, visiting WCCO at least twice a week. The girls always left with a big box of mail, although they had an ulterior motive for checking their correspondence frequently. Julie confessed, "We love to stop at the mail room because there's a super cute guy working in there!"

Reveling in their new status, Julie and Carol were even permitted to sit in on taping sessions of the *Axel* show. They were thrilled by how nice everyone at the station was. Tom Cousins always seemed to have time for them; Jim Oliverson of the Promotion Department helped them with the club's paper; floor manager Stan Wolfson let them look through a television camera; the two stars of the show talked and joked with them. Julie wrote in amazement, "I can't believe we really know Mary Davies and Clellan Card!! It seems like a dream."

One day after a show, Carol and Julie wanted to ask Clellan something, so they hurried down the narrow hallway off Studio 4 that led to the storeroom that served as Clell's dressing room. The door was open and Julie burst in, just in time to see Clellan about to unzip his pants. Shrieking in surprise and embarrassment, she turned around so abruptly that she knocked Carol down the steps, and then fell on top of her. Fortunately, neither of them were hurt. Julie started laughing so hard she thought she was crying. "C'mon in, girls, I'm decent," Clellan said, roaring with laughter himself. "If you would have been a minute later, there really would have been some excitement!"

The girls stayed busy producing the *Tree House Tribune* every month. In April 1965, Carol and Julie interviewed Clellan and Mary to gather material for full-page biographies which appeared in the paper's fourth issue. Clellan described himself as "lovable" and "sweet-smelling." The article also noted, "He spends much of his spare time thinking up different places to loaf. He likes to eat outdoors, play golf, and swim under water. Some of Clellan's favor-

What do you think this is, Mary – Christmas?

ites include the color red (that's the reason for the red stripes on his shirt), jazz music, and his favorite food is steak. He has two dogs and 'a couple of mice in the basement.'"

The following month, the *Tree House Tribune* kicked off Axel's campaign for president of Magic Island. "Big, strong, courageous, mighty, rugged, masculine" Axel was up against "low down, sneaky, scheming, weakling" Sam Sapolio. Sam apparently was a good-looking dog, but except for his many character flaws almost nothing else is known about him; he remained a mysterious, shadowy figure. However, he was relentlessly denigrated in the *Tree House Tribune*, while Axel was praised as someone who stood for "everything that's good in life." The Scandinavian scalawag turned out to be a shrewd politician. His platform was designed to please both his young constituency and his television sponsors, promising "a Tonka Toy in every sandbox, boneless Hectors Nector [*sic*] in every pot, Axel's Safety Stickers on every car and bike, Peters Wieners in every kettle."

> Some of the other things he stands for are an up with every down, an in with every out, a T with every V, a rabbit with every foot, a bath with every tub, a bird with every bath, a cookie with every jar, a milk with every shake, a banana with every split, a gum with every drop, a lamp with every shade, a pop with every sicle, a jack in every box, a bounce in every ball, a pop with every corn, a coffee with every pot, a moon with every beam, a candy with every cane, a rag in every bag, and a sun with every shine.

Naturally, Carmen was the vice presidential candidate on Axel's ticket and Tallulah vied for the number two spot on Sam's side. Despite the blatant favoritism, the election was alleged to be very close. On Wednesday, June 30, 1965, Julie and Carol appeared on the *Axel* show for the second time, serving as vote tabulators. As the votes "came in," the girls walked onto the set and recorded them on a blackboard. Each time they did, Axel or Carmen would say something about "who's getting the most marks." The election was purported to be a dead heat until finally, Nosecone Needleman cast the deciding vote. (Confidentially, the whole thing was probably rigged from the very beginning.)

The next day, there was a big victory celebration in the tree house. Julie and Carol brought streamers and confetti, a banner for Axel that

What's that in the road – a head?

Carmen and Axel celebrate their birthdays with Julie and Carol in June 1965

read "President," and roses for Carmen. During the show, the girls and the cameramen threw confetti at the president-elect and his running mate as they sang their theme song, "On Sisconsin!"

Just a few days earlier, there had been another shindig in Axel's aerie. Because Clellan and Mary had birthdays in June that fell just two days apart, Julie and Carol had decided to throw them a party. On Monday, June 28, 1965, they brought a variety of treats down to the studio. The girls decorated the tree house with a big "Happy Birthday!" banner, covered the table with a festive paper tablecloth, and placed a couple of gaily wrapped gifts among the food. During the merrymaking, Axel sported a gigantic "Axel President" medallion on his chest, and Carmen wore an eccentric homemade corsage. As the four principals of the Axel and Carmen Fan Club munched happily on cookies and cupcakes, none of them had any inkling that they were celebrating Clellan's last birthday.

Clellan Card

CHAPTER 20

"Tell 'Em I'M GoING AROUNd THE WORLD"

DURING 1965, the decline in Clellan's health began to accelerate. In February, it became quite evident that his lymph nodes were larger, an indication that his cancer was growing. Still, he felt well enough to go on a trip which had been in the works for months. He had been recruited as the host of a Caribbean cruise, heading a group of about 120 people (including Marion, and cousin Bill Card and his wife, Mailand) bent on escaping the Minnesota winter. They sailed out of Port Everglades, Florida, aboard the Cunard Lines ship the R. M. S. Carmania (!) on February 27 (which is why Axel wasn't present for the inauguration of the Fan Club two days later).

The ship stopped at Port-au-Prince in Haiti, Curacao, and Barbados, among other exotic locales. Unsurprisingly, Clellan turned out to be an outstanding host, emceeing evening programs aboard ship and generally keeping everyone happy. "Clellan was just so naturally friendly," cruise organizer Dennis Blenis said. "He'd be 'on' when he was up at the microphone, but he'd be 'on' visiting the people around the ship, too. They really learned to love him." He even taught Dennis the finer points of pie throwing during the excursion. After enjoying a fun-filled two weeks, the group returned home on March 14.

At the end of March, though, Clellan's legs abruptly began to swell up, a worrisome sign of his cancer's progression. He was admitted to Abbott Hospital for treatment. After a couple of days, his condition improved so he was discharged. His health continued to slide, however, prompting further tests in July. The diagnosis revealed that his lymphoma, relatively benign for years, had metamorphosed into a much more aggressive form of the disease. The news amounted to a death sentence.

In one of life's bittersweet ironies, Clellan's second grandchild, Michael Scott Card, was born in California on July 14, 1965, just two days after his grim diagnosis. (Mary Colleen, the first grandchild, had been born on November 5, 1962.) The proud grandparents traveled to California for a visit as soon as they could. The family reunion, though happy, was clouded by Clellan's ill health. "My dad was sick by that time," the elder Michael related. "When it was time for them to leave for the airport, they insisted we put them on the airport bus behind the Biltmore Hotel. That was the last time I saw my father alive. The irony – it's almost Twilight Zone sort of stuff – is that was the same place that my parents and I said goodbye to my brother John for the last time."

Despite his illness, for much of the year Clellan's life went on more or less normally. As he had since 1955, Axel appeared in the

The 1965 WCCO-TV Aquatennial float with (L to R) news anchor Dave Moore, Allan Lotsberg as Willie Ketchem, weatherman Bud Kraehling, entertainment reporter Bill Carlson, and Clellan Card as Axel

Aquatennial parade on Saturday, July 17, waving his giant comb. Carmen, Clancy, Willie Ketchem, and other WCCO-TV personalities also rode on the station's blue and white float, but it was Axel who got the biggest response from the crowd.

Events like these parades drove home to Allan Lotsberg what it meant to be the idol of thousands of kids. He recalled with amazement, "It's 85 in the middle of summer and we wave and wave, and we hear them yelling – there's a high that comes with that. Just throngs of people shouting your *name*."

Axel continued making personal appearances, still willing to show up almost anywhere – even for free, if it was for a good cause. In August, for example, he attended a backyard carnival held to raise money for the fight against multiple sclerosis. Corey Gordon, the eight-year-old who organized the event, remembered anxiously waiting for Axel with his brother and mother while the carnival was going on in the backyard. Axel, decked out in his costume, arrived on time and chatted briefly with the Gordons before making his way towards the backyard along the side of the house.

"One way to describe it is Pied Piper-like," Corey recalled. "By the time we got to the side of the house, there was already a mob of kids starting to swarm around him. I just have one of these vivid, vivid pictures of him being *mobbed*. You know, just swarms of kids all completely around him and having to kind of wade through, shaking hands, and giving out autographs, and just chitchatting with kids, answering questions. He didn't get very far into the backyard because there was a significant mob of people." Axel wasn't there long, maybe twenty minutes or so; after munching on a hot dog and playing a ring toss game or two, he departed – but he left behind a crowd of very thrilled kids.

Axel and Carmen interview Minnesota governor Carl Rolvaag at the State Fair in 1965

The *Axel* program continued much as it had for years, although occasionally Mary was too busy to appear. At such times, Allan Lotsberg's character Willie Ketchem often

 How do you like your homemade butter – Pat?

took her place. Accustomed to John Gallos's low-key Clancy persona, Allan didn't quite know what to make of Clell's more caustic
humor. He remembered that Axel often introduced Willie by saying
something like, "Carmen is a tree surgeon and she's busy with a new
patient, so I got El Shrimpo here today."

A typical encounter involved Axel describing Willie's duties
around the tree house: "If you're wondering what diss guy's doing
here," he would say, "I use him to take the squeaks and rattles out of
my car. That's what he does here." Then, turning to the hapless Willie, "So, go get rid of some squeaks and rattles, will ya, and I'll call ya
in as time allows."

Perhaps Clellan was hoping that Willie would give Axel a snappy
comeback, the way Don Stolz had, but that just wasn't Allan's style.
"He'd dismiss me," Allan said, "and so I'd say 'Okay, okay,' and I'd
walk away. Then I'd come back and hope I could get on a little bit
later." The kidvid star chuckled at the memory. "He just browbeat me
to death. A classic curmudgeon is what he was. He'd dismiss you in a
minute, and at the same time, you'd say, 'Hey, I just got put down by
Axel! I feel real good about that!' So he got away with it."

Clellan could even get away with joking at a funeral. A case in
point was the Catholic requiem for his friend, Ed Viehman. A slew of
Knights of Columbus attended, decked out in their full regalia. At a
certain point in the Mass, they all drew their swords in unison. At
that moment, Clellan, one of the pallbearers, leaned over to Wayne
Fields, another pallbearer, and whispered, "Watch it, Wayne! They
know you're a Protestant!"

In another of life's little ironies, Clellan was given a brand-new
work assignment in the twilight of his career. On Wednesday, September 15, 1965, he began as the moderator of *Roundy Predicts*, a
sports prognostication program.[26] In addition to star prophet Roundy
Coughlin, the show that year also featured old hand Halsey Hall and
longtime newspaper columnist Dick Cullum. Clellan, the die-hard
sports fan, undoubtedly relished trading opinions and tall tales with
his three fellow veterans. Coach Teakwood Torgeson may even have
lurched on-screen occasionally.

At the end of November, however, Clellan's health took another
turn for the worse. His legs swelled up again, and there were signs
that his lymphoma was spreading. On December 1, he was admitted

to Abbott Hospital for another round of treatments. His condition seemed to improve, and so he was discharged after two days. By this time, Clellan's illness had become quite apparent to his co-workers. He'd lost a great deal of weight, eventually plunging from more than 200 pounds to less than 120, and looked quite frail. With the decline in his health, Clellan – a private person anyway – grew more and more withdrawn. "He became very remote," Mary remembered. "He didn't want to see people, he didn't want to talk to people."

"I used to bump into him in the lobby when he'd come back from chemotherapy," Allan Lotsberg recalled. "His face would be all ashen, and he'd be tired, and I'd say, 'Clell, you look like you're looking for somebody's trike to kick.' And he'd say, 'You bet I am.' He just was wearing down – he got kind of grumpy toward the end."

Clellan did his best to ensure that his young fans didn't see the darker side of his life. Even Julie and Carol, the ubiquitous co-presidents of the Axel and Carmen Fan Club, remained oblivious to how serious his condition was. As far as the two girls knew, everything was fine – better than ever, in fact. Beginning in December 1965, Axel and Carmen wrote their own columns for the *Tree House Tribune*. Unfortunately, this proved to be a short-lived novelty. Axel penned his final installment for the February 1966 issue:

Hi Kiddoes –

Hope you all are happy and healthy and are minding papa and mama or big sister or auntie or uncle or whoever takes care of you.

I was thinking about our big carnival last year in the forest when we had lots of contests and games and pop corn and hot dogs and all kinds of goodies to eat. And the prizes – WOW! Like two dozen Rooster's eggs, a big bag full of donut holes, fried ice, two pounds of Johnson grass, and a second-hand hardly used fingernail clipper. And the second prize – how wonderful that was! The guy that won second prize got to kiss Carmen Kissleman! What was first prize? Oh, the first prize was ten cents.

I'd like to have another carnival, wouldn't you?

Love and kisses,

Axel

In early 1966, Clellan's health began to deteriorate dramatically. His hospitalizations became more and more frequent. After suffering through another series of cancer treatments in February, he was discharged from Abbott Hospital on the 26th, only to be re-admitted early in March for more treatments. He was discharged again on March 11. Ever the trouper, Clell continued to do the show between hospital visits and bouts of chemotherapy. "He tried so hard to keep going," Mary remarked with a mixture of admiration and melancholy. Ultimately, though, the reality of his situation was inescapable.

One day, probably in the third or fourth week of March 1966, Clellan came in to do the show, but found that he was physically unable to continue. He knew that he'd finally reached the end of the line. As he slowly made his way off the set, he told Mary flatly, "I won't be back."

She'd been dreading the moment for some time, but when it finally came, she became very distraught. "What should I do?" she implored him. "What do you want me to tell the kids?"

"Aah, tell 'em I'm going around the world," he grumbled, and walked away. Remembering the moment, Mary murmured sadly, "That was the last time I saw him."

Even at this juncture, with his illness entering its final stages, Clellan was still willing to make time for his young fans. Thirteen-year-old Larry Stelter was in Fairview Hospital for a few days and, out of boredom, began flipping through the phone book. He happened upon Clellan's name and impulsively dialed his home number. When Clellan answered, Larry asked if he was Axel. "Yes, I am," came the reply. An excited Larry and the three other kids in the hospital room spent nearly forty-five minutes talking to him, never suspecting how precarious their TV hero's own health had become.

Clellan began a final round of hospitalizations not long after, entering Abbott yet again in late March. He checked out on Saturday, April 2, but just three days later, on Tuesday, April 5, he returned to Abbott Hospital for the last time. "I remember very vividly seeing Clellan about a week before he died," said Toby Prin's son, David. "He was extremely ill. It was clear that he was down to a shadow of himself. His personality was very sublimated. We talked for maybe five, ten minutes – and he was still cordial – but clearly, it was not an appropriate time to spend much time with him."

Fellow broadcaster Bob DeHaven also visited, but it was an uncomfortable get-together for the two old friends. Standing at the foot of the bed, Bob feebly protested that, in the hospital, company really isn't welcome. Clellan emphatically agreed, launching into a tirade about visitors talking, laughing, using his telephone, and generally annoying him. Nonplussed, Bob soon left.[27]

In that drab and antiseptic hospital room, however, one person was never far from Clellan's side: Marion. For nearly 44 years, her husband had given her "oceans of love," and she had returned that love in kind. Together, the two of them had enjoyed sublime happiness and endured unspeakable tragedy – but their shared journey was nearly at an end.

Although the treatments seemed to have little effect on the inexorable progress of Clellan's lymphoma, his doctors nevertheless renewed their assault on his cancer. Unfortunately, the cure may have been worse than the disease. Higher and higher doses of radiation sapped his strength, while the chemotherapy reduced his white blood cell count to a point where he could no longer effectively fight infections. The human body is always prey to a plethora of bacteria, but under normal circumstances, its defenses can keep germs at bay. However, in his weakened state, Clellan no longer could. He was apparently overwhelmed by septicemia, more commonly known as blood poisoning. He went into shock and sank into a coma. Finally, at 10:05 A.M. on Wednesday, April 13, 1966, Clellan Card died.

"It was relatively quick," his son Michael said, his voice tinged with regret. That final morning, Marion had called Michael at work to tell him that his father probably would not survive the day. He dropped everything and grabbed the first available flight to Minneapolis. As soon as he got off the airplane, he called the hospital, only to be told that his dad had passed away. He took a taxi to his parents' house in Excelsior, numb with shock. "I had no baggage," Michael recalled, "and I was walking towards the front door, and Bob DeHaven was walking the other way. Bob just looked at me and shook his head and kept walking. I can't remember anything after that."

Many of Clellan's friends and fans were also overcome with grief. Julie Moden, co-president of the Axel and Carmen Fan Club, put her feelings in writing:

> *Today is the worst day of my life. Axel died today. He had cancer. Carol & I didn't even know how sick he was until Tom told us just a little while ago. We hadn't seen him at the studio in a while & sometimes when we*

were down [there] people would talk softly to Carmen. We thought there might be something wrong but I guess no one wanted to be the one to tell us.

Because of Axel I've just had the most fun year of my life. He can't be gone. I won't believe he's dead. He was a friend to thousands & my special friend & friends don't leave. Axel, I know that you didn't die but just moved on to another tree house in a much taller tree where you can greet the birdie with the yellow bill every morning. You'll always live on Magic Island and in my heart. I love you Axel.

Most Twin Cities youngsters couldn't even remember a world without Axel. Bob Pratt, born in 1954, recalled, "I probably started watching TV when I was four or five, so as far as I was concerned, Axel had *always* been there. That's why when he *wasn't*, it was a pretty tough thing for a kid to deal with. At that point in my life, I'd never had anybody close to me die."

Mary Davies was especially heartbroken. She had worked with Clellan for nearly two decades, for the last few years on a daily basis. "The only person I remember grieving more for was my father," she said. "Clellan really was a larger-than-life person. The day he died was a very difficult day for me. We all knew Clellan was dying when we were doing the show, and Carmen, as a result, was dying too. My little alter ego was dying along with Clellan. When he died, I assumed the show would be over."

However, that same day Harry called Mary and told her, "They want you to come in and do the show tomorrow." Mary was a bit taken aback. She said, "Well, don't you think we should bury the man and give this some time?"

"No," he replied. "[Station manager] Sherm Headley just called and said he wants you to continue the show." Harry's inclination was to simply go on with the program as if nothing had happened, but Mary insisted on making a public statement of some sort.

The next morning, the program began cold, without the customary theme music. Carmen appeared on-screen and solemnly told viewers that Axel had gone away and would not be able to come back. Exercising a restraint that seems almost quaint today, she avoided any specific mention of death to minimize the trauma for her young audience. She went on to say that she thought that Axel would want them to continue meeting in the tree house, enjoying

The Little Rascals and having fun. She told the kids that she would do the show as long as they wanted her to do it.

In a similar vein, "A Note from Carmen" appeared in the *Tree House Tribune* in June:

Dear Kids,

For just a minute, I'd like to be serious and thank the many of you who took the time to write to me in the Treehouse and to Mrs. Card, Axel's wife, when Axel passed away. It shows how kind and thoughtful even little people can be.

Many have written saying they are glad Carmen will stay in the Treehouse, and although it is a big responsibility for Carmen to do a good show for you kids, I'm happy to be with you still and we'll have some good times. Thank you for wanting me.

On Thursday afternoon, the day after Clellan's death, visitation began in the Huber-Lee funeral home in Excelsior. A prayer service was conducted there on Friday evening, with much laughter afterwards as family and friends reminisced about the beloved broadcaster. The funeral itself was held at 10:00 A.M. on Saturday, April 16, at St. John the Baptist Catholic Church in Excelsior. It was a beautiful spring day, and the church was crowded with relatives, friends, and fans. Father Oscar Winzerling, pastor, said the Requiem Mass. The pallbearers were mostly Clellan's colleagues from television and radio: Don Stolz, Harry Jones, Bob DeHaven, WCCO-TV newscaster Dean Montgomery, friend Dennis Blenis, and Excelsior neighbor Bob Armstrong. There was a private interment at Resurrection Cemetery, where Clellan was laid to rest alongside his two sons. His headstone was a simple one, matching those of Peter and John. Following the service, a reception was held at the Cards' house on MacLynn Road, where again the sadness was alleviated somewhat by friends sharing many fond and funny memories.

Once the initial shock had passed, the family had to confront the legal and financial realities of their situation. They discovered that Clellan had anticipated their needs. "Everything was in order," Michael remembered. "He had everything all set up before he died, because he knew he was going to go, he just didn't know when – but he knew it was going to be soon. He had all of his papers put together, all of his life insurance, everything was all bang, bang, bang. All we

had to do was open up the drawer and there it was. That's how he spent his time before he died."

In response to many inquiries in the wake of Clellan's death, both divisions of WCCO established a Clellan Card Memorial Fund to raise money for cancer research. Just three months after Clellan's passing, the fund had grown to an impressive $5,630. About half of the total had been contributed by children, who sent in their quarters, dimes, nickels, and pennies. Many of the youngsters wrote that they had emptied their piggy banks or had earned the money through various projects. The balance was donated by the eleven McDonald's restaurants in the Twin Cities area that had held a Clellan Card Memorial Fund Day on July 12.

Mary Davies, John Gallos, and Allan Lotsberg presented the money to the University of Minnesota Hospital, along with a commemorative plaque. The bulk of the money was used to buy a $4,000 Coulter counter for leukemia research conducted by the Department of Pediatrics at the University of Minnesota. The remainder went to support other research by the University's pediatrics department.

It was a fitting way to remember a man who had done so much for children during his lifetime, but perhaps Clellan himself offered the best epitaph. In his final "One Man's Opinion" column for the *Minnetonka Record* newspaper, he closed with a quotation from Zane Grey:

> *To bear up under loss – to fight the bitterness of defeat and the weakness of grief – to be victor over anger – to smile when tears are close – to resist evil men and base instincts – to hate hate and love love – to go on when it would seem good to die – to seek ever after the glory and the dream – to look up with unquenchable faith in something ever more about to be – that is what any man can do, and so be great.*

One such man was Clellan Card.

John Gallos as Clancy the Cop, Mary Davies as Carmen the Nurse, and Allan Lotsberg as Willie Ketchem, circa 1967

AFTERWARD

IN THE YEARS immediately after Clellan's death, live-action children's shows remained profitable for local stations. Although the networks had discovered that they could make more money on cartoons than on comparatively expensive live children's television productions, it was another story at hometown affiliates. A low-budget children's show still made financial sense for provincial stations. Sponsors clamored to get their products onto the kids' shows. They loved having local hosts announce their commercials because they were incredibly effective hucksters, or children were incredibly gullible consumers – or perhaps a bit of both. In any case, when products were promoted by local kidvid favorites, multitudes of kids bought them.

Some saw this as exploitation. A group of concerned parents formed Action for Children's Television (ACT), spearheading an effort to clean up kids' TV. To protect children from all sorts of alleged evils, ACT pressured the National Association of Broadcasters to enact sweeping reforms. Finally, in 1972, the NAB Code was amended to say:

> Children's program hosts or primary cartoon characters shall not be utilized to deliver commercial messages within or adjacent to the programs which feature such hosts or cartoon characters. This provision shall also apply to lead-ins to commercials when such lead-ins contain sell copy or employ endorsement of the product by program host or primary cartoon characters.

This amendment became effective on January 1, 1973. Even though the NAB Code was a collection of nonbinding principles that

I hear you got a new tractor – lug!

stations abided by in a rather desultory fashion, in this case compliance was assured because no one wanted to appear to be taking advantage of children.

Although the directive didn't eliminate commercials from kids' shows, in one stroke it erased the reason sponsors had supported local kiddie show hosts. Since those hosts could not endorse or even introduce products, they were of no use to advertisers anymore. Lack of interest from sponsors, in turn, meant that TV stations no longer had a financial incentive to go to the trouble of mounting a daily or weekly children's production. Local stations could fill airtime with relatively cheap cartoons, just as the networks already had, or with syndicated programs that had no regional connection.

Unfortunately but not unexpectedly, local television stations put making money ahead of fostering a sense of community – and broadcast regulators failed to take steps to ensure that stations kept their children's shows on the air. Instead, the NAB rules made those shows economically unviable and, without a government mandate to continue producing such programs, virtually guaranteed that they would vanish. And from coast to coast, the shows *did* vanish, in droves. By the end of the 1970s, local children's television was dead in all but a few markets where the public absolutely refused to let their cherished programs disappear. Eventually, however, even those venerable institutions expired, and they were not replaced. Today, virtually everywhere in the United States, local children's television programming is extinct.

In the Twin Cities, the impact of the new commercial regulations was immediate and unmistakeable: after almost nineteen years on the air, Channel 11's *Lunch with Casey* was summarily cancelled. Roger Awsumb, who starred as serene engineer Casey Jones, and Lynn Dwyer, his manic sidekick Roundhouse Rodney, had been rendered utterly expendable to Metromedia, Inc., the conglomerate which then owned WTCN-TV. A storm of protest from the local community ensued, but Metromedia stood fast. Casey pulled into the station for the final time at noon on Friday December 29, 1972, just days before the NAB amendment was due to take effect.

It was a bittersweet finale. Regular chef Hank Meadows gave Casey a pumpkin pie, animal man Bob Duerr presented him with a mounted South American butterfly, and Minnesota Twins legend

 What kind of car are you driving, Abe – Lincoln?

Harmon Killebrew "poked in his balding head to mutter a farewell." People from the Como Zoo brought Billy the monkey and Peaches the skunk to say good-bye; Billy expressed his condolences by stomping through the pie.

Minneapolis mayor Charles Stenvig put in a surprise appearance, toting a bag of McDonald's hamburgers. He announced that he had signed a "Bring Back Casey" petition, which unfortunately had no impact whatsoever. Hizzoner promised Casey a distinguished service award, chomped on a burger, and departed.

After reading the list of kids' birthdays for the final time, Roundhouse and Casey bid their audience farewell. Roundhouse declared, "To all the gang out there, if we caused you to laugh a little, we were pleased. If we got you to learn something, we were honored. But if we caused you to *think*, then this has been perfect."

Finally, it was Casey's turn. "Well, it's been a long time. Thanks to everybody here and I hope we'll see you," he said, his voice breaking. "Just thank you all very much." An audience had accumulated in the studio as the show progressed, and at the end they burst into applause. After the broadcast, Roger Awsumb quit his other job as WTCN-TV's booth announcer and left the station forever.

To its credit, WCCO-TV hung on to its children's shows a bit longer, despite the prohibition on endorsements. However, the same forces that had relegated local kidvid to the early morning ghetto

Roger Awsumb as Casey Jones and Lynn Dwyer as Roundhouse Rodney

inexorably continued to build until the shows were pushed off the air completely. Production costs were spiraling higher and, to put it bluntly, most television time became too valuable to waste on kids.

At Channel 4, the end came suddenly. One day, the station announced the wholesale cancellation of its long-running children's programs to make way for the hot *Donahue* show. Mary Davies, John Gallos, and Allan Lotsberg – all of whom had been at the station for fifteen years or more – were required to audition for a single new kiddie host position. Allan Lotsberg got the nod, so the kidvid careers of Mary Davies and John Gallos were finished.

On March 25, 1977, *Carmen* and *Clancy and Willie* made their exit. In the opening of Carmen's final show, as her theme song "Be a Friend" played, the *Carmen* title graphic was emblazoned on the screen. Normally a virginal white, on the last day the lettering was a funeral black. Carmen shuffled stiffly onto the set, her eyes puffy. "Good morning, Carmen!" announcer Bud Kraehling said brightly. "What's happening in the cottage today?"

"It's a very special day on Magic Island," she declared without enthusiasm, "and I'll get to that with a little story for you later." Following a *Little Rascals* episode (Yep, they were still there!) and a couple of uninspired segments, Carmen, seated at her desk, told a little fable: "About twenty-seven years ago, a beautiful young girl wandered into WCCO television, walked over to a piano, and started singing a song on a show, and immediately fell in love, not only with the people on that show, but with people on many, many shows to come.

"And that beautiful young girl is still beautiful," she paused and sniffed with exaggerated hauteur, "albeit long in the tooth. However, twenty-seven years is a long, long time to have a wonderful time and a wonderful love affair with great and wonderful people. I am the gal who came in, and today is the day that I am going to leave WCCO television, and I will be leaving as Carmen. I'm going to miss you, and I know you'll miss Carmen, but that's the way it goes. Time moves on."

Carmen recounted a brief version of how she got started on *Axel and His Dog*, praising Harry Jones, "a wonderful, talented, creative man. It is to him I owe all my thanks for a wonderful, happy career." Then, without any preamble, she said, "Clellan Card became ill, many years ago, about eleven years ago, and we lost him." Her words became rushed, her voice rising in pitch. "I was fortunate enough to continue to be Carmen and join you kids every morning for all this fun."

"Well, times change, kids," she declared. "Things move along. You're going to learn as you grow up that never do things stay the same. But I will be happy to remember that I am probably the longest-term children's personality in the Twin Cities area. For twenty-four years[28] I've been coming to you as Carmen the Nurse, and loving you and loving to be with you, and loving everybody connected with Carmen, and the Cottage, and the tree house." She thanked the crew and staff who "make this station the wonderful station that it is and will continue to be."

"There is so much I could say," she continued, smiling bravely, "and there's so much love I would like to express, but most of it for those daddies and moms who were little kids twenty-four years ago when Carmen came to join you for the first time, who now have little kids themselves. I just want to say 'Thank you.' In all the years I've been Carmen, I think I've received maybe eight letters that were critical or unkind. That's quite a record for this length of time."

Steeling herself, she went into the wind-up. "WCCO television, that's the place to stay. 7:00 to 7:30, be here with Allan Lotsberg and Willie Ketchem, in all the years to come. God bless you. I love you." She blew a kiss and abruptly got up from her desk. As she quickly walked off the set, she called out plaintively, "Remember me!"

Following a commercial break, the final installment of *Clancy and Willie* began. The two stars got things rolling by singing a quick rendition of "Good Morning" from the movie *Singin' in the Rain*, their traditional opening since moving to the early morning time slot. The centerpiece of that last program was Clancy's histrionic telling of "Casey at the Bat." John Gallos had memorized the poem when he was eight years old, and Clancy's rendition was a recurrent highlight of the show.

Finally, though, the inevitable could not be postponed any longer. Typically, near the end of the program Clancy and Willie would talk to the kids in the Peanut Gallery, but on this melancholy occasion there was no studio audience. Instead, Willie soberly informed viewers, "This is the last day. We are closing the Agency here at old WCCO

I don't want none of your sass – Parilla!

Television." He mentioned his new show, scheduled to begin the following Monday, thanked the kids for watching, and then yielded the floor to Clancy.

More accurately, he yielded to John Gallos, who gave the valedictory speech. "It has been a real pleasure and a privilege to have been a part of many of the routines in many homes around the Twin Cities, and Minnesota and Wisconsin, for lo, these past many years," he declared. "And, as you close out twenty years of children's programming, I guess your thoughts go back to many people, many friends who have helped you along the way.

"Certainly, one of those is the man who just talked to you: Allan Lotsberg, who's been a very talented and a very fine performer, and who's been very helpful down through the years.

"Another man who comes to mind is the gentleman who started me out on the road to children's programming, way back in the year 1957, exactly twenty years ago here on Channel 4: he's the director of the Old Log Theater, Mr. Don Stolz. Don Stolz's encouragement and advice, rehearsals and training, had a lot to do with much of the longevity that I have been able to enjoy here over the past twenty years entertaining children on Channel 4. And certainly I want to thank him also.

"Also a very important person who has done so much to sustain me in the ups and downs that it takes to run a television program over twenty years is our executive producer, Harry Jones, who has always been a friend and who's always had us strive for excellence on this program, and I think occasionally we even achieved it.

"We've had a lot of laughs over the years, we've had some ups, we've had some downs – and it isn't over yet, because I know I'll be looking for you on other programs here on Channel 4. I'd like to close with an Irish blessing that I think Clancy would enjoy:

Wishing you always
Walls for the wind
And a roof for the rain
And tea beside the fire.
Laughter to cheer you
And those you love near you
And all that your heart might desire.
May the road rise to meet you

May the wind be always at your back
May the rains fall soft upon your fields
And until we meet again,
May God hold you in the palm of his hand.

As he recited the verse, the camera slowly moved in, until at the finish Clancy's face filled the screen. He gazed steadily into the lens, forced a sad little smile, and said simply, "Good-bye."

It was the end of an era. Allan Lotsberg's program, titled *Allan's Window*, was the very last gasp of Twin Cities children's television. Allan opted to appear on it as himself, rather than in the guise of Willie Ketchem, and gave the show an educational bent. Broadcast for two years, *Allan's Window* was sidelined in 1979 by a labor dispute at the station. Once the strike was settled, however, Allan was curtly informed that his services were no longer required. His show never aired again.

"Outside of the news, weather, and sports," Dave Moore lamented, "there is no local production of any kind these days, has *not* been for many, many years, and the attitude that I've been able to glean from most of the executives of local broadcasting is there will not *be* any local programming in days to come."

Something of real value was lost when local children's television programming ceased to exist. Even very young children seemed to realize that there was something different about their homegrown programs. *Howdy Doody* or *Captain Kangaroo* might have been a favorite, but kids understood that a show like *Axel and His Dog* really *belonged* to them in a way that the network programs never would. And as Roger Awsumb pointed out many times in later years, a cartoon can't visit a school, or a hospital, or a church. But people like Roger and Clellan could – and did, hundreds (if not thousands) of times.

Early on, John Gallos was struck by the realization that he and his compatriots "really were a force in the lives of these kids. I would run into kids from borderline areas, the poor neighborhoods. Their noses were runny, their clothes were dirty, and, God, you know some of these kids were probably abused in some way. You could just tell. They clung to you. They weren't getting enough love at home, see. So they relied on a TV character to provide a little love."

Following Clellan's death, Marion moved out of their house in

 What did you do with that big lemon – squeezer?

Excelsior. Totally unsentimental about possessions – perhaps in an effort to discard reminders of happy days that were gone forever – she sold Clellan's extensive record collection and many other items that he had accumulated. She eventually relocated to a condominium in the Minneapolis suburb of Edina, where she spent her last years enjoying such things as canasta with a small circle of friends. Like many people of her generation, she was stoic and rarely complained about anything that may have been bothering her, either physically or emotionally. Instead, she simply suffered in silence.

Sadly, she had all too much to suffer. Not only did she lose two of her three children, five of her seven siblings also preceded her in death. And before her own passing, she and her only remaining son experienced yet another terrible loss. In 1978, Michael's eldest child, Mary Colleen, was severely injured in a bicycle accident at the age of fifteen. After sustaining her on life support for some time in the hope of a miracle, on June 27th the decision was finally made to disconnect the machinery and let her go.

But through it all, Marion's faith sustained her. She often prayed in private and yet was resigned to whatever life had in store for her. Frequently sad though not morose, she didn't necessarily wish to die herself after Clellan passed away, but she certainly looked forward to joining him and her boys in the next life.

In the months preceding her death, Marion had fainting spells during which she would nod off and be "out" for a few seconds, then awake and be fine. On October 15, 1979, she nodded out and did not revive. No attempt was made to resuscitate her, in accordance with her wishes.

Despite enduring more than his share of tragedy, Clellan and Marion's son, Michael, has nonetheless managed to forge a happy life in southern California with his wife, Elizabeth, working as a commercial real estate developer and consultant. Their daughter, Terrill Anne, lives nearby with her husband and their two young children. Michael's son, Mike, lives near Los Angeles with his wife and twin boys and works with a freight forwarding company.

After *Carmen* went off the air, Mary Davies continued her singing career, although she complained bitterly that it had been derailed by WCCO-TV when it was announced that she had "retired" when her show ended. Not unprepared, she sold real estate for a time, and then

Jerry Mayeron, Mary Davies, and Harry Jones in 2004, at Mary's induction into the Pavek Museum of Broadcasting's Hall of Fame

specialized in property management. When she and her husband, Robert Orfield, actually did retire, they moved to their lake home in Nevis, Minnesota, and enjoyed many happy years together there. Robert's declining health eventually necessitated their return to the Twin Cities, where he died on February 15, 1997.

Harry Jones, the guiding hand of most of Channel 4's children's shows, continued to head the station's film department after the demise of the children's programs. Eventually he also began producing and directing commercials for the station's subsidiary, Production 4 Studios. He retired from WCCO-TV in 1986, occasionally freelancing as a lighting director. In November 1996, he lost his wife Jo after a long illness. They first met at Channel 4, in the days when it was known as WTCN-TV, and had been married for nearly forty years. On June 14, 2008, Harry also passed away, at the age of 83.

Don and Joan Stolz purchased the Old Log property from long-time landlord Harry Kuechle in May 1968. Over the years, stars such as Lois Nettleton, Nick Nolte, and Loni Anderson trod the boards at the Old Log on their way to bigger things, but many others stayed to help make the theater an enduring part of the Twin Cities' cultural

Joan and Don Stolz

milieu. The theater that was born in a stable is still going strong after more than six decades but Don's beloved Joan, his wife for sixty-four years, died of leukemia on September 16, 2007.

A number of Clellan's co-workers and fellow broadcasters have also passed on. Among the most notable: Mel Jass died of heart failure on January 20, 1997; Dave Moore succumbed after a long illness on January 23, 1998; Roger Awsumb expired due to cardiac arrest near Brainerd, Minnesota, on July 15, 2002 (ironically the same area where his TV partner Lynn Dwyer met his premature end from the same cause in 1976); pneumonia took Jimmy Valentine on December 5, 2002; and John Gallos died of complications from diabetes on November 15, 2005.

Clellan Card may have died, but countless Minnesotans still remember vividly the radio jokester who was such an indelible part of every morning, the mellow-voiced disc jockey with his encyclopedic musical knowledge, and most of all, the goofy Scandihoovian hermit who somehow became the friend of thousands of kids. Axel struck a chord with his audience that resonates long after his death.

Corey Gordon, the organizer of the backyard carnival against MS that Axel had attended in 1965, decided to redirect his fund-raising efforts to the Clellan Card Memorial Fund of the American Cancer Society. As it turned out, that opened a lot of doors: local companies couldn't do enough to memorialize Clellan. Tonka Toys, which had declined to make any donations to the MS carnival, suddenly became incredibly generous, contributing huge cases of toys. Before long, word got around that Corey's carnival had some great prizes to offer. In 1966, the event garnered $121 for the cause; by 1970, the final year, the total approached $2,000.

In 1975, two young promoters, Louis Bohl and Don Olson, staged "A Salute to the Fabulous Fifties" at St. Cloud State College and the Minneapolis Auditorium. In addition to showing a complete Axel program on film, the extravaganza featured Mary Davies reminiscing about her days with Axel and singing songs of the 1950s with the band The Rockin' Hollywoods.

WCCO-TV commemorated the tenth anniversary of Clellan's death with a locally produced special called *Clellan Card's Humor*, shown on September 20, 1976. The program was the brainchild of Kathleen Abel, a recent graduate of Augsburg College. WCCO-TV director Dan Silverman, a guest lecturer at the college, had learned of Kathleen's interest in children's programming and invited her down to the station to meet Harry Jones. Out of curiosity, she asked Harry if the station had any film of Axel. Told that it did, she began to formulate the idea of a tribute special.

When broadcast, the show consisted of *Axel and His Dog* film clips interspersed with the recollections of Don Stolz, Mary Davies, and Harry Jones. Many rare photographs, as well as a portion of one of Clellan's radio shows, were also included. Although Axel's original set no longer existed, the environs of Axel's Tree House were re-created for the special. A moment of poignant nostalgia came when Don and Mary, visibly moved, took their familiar places at the crotch of the tree. Kathleen herself made an appearance near the end of the program to share her own memories of Axel.

Axel still occasionally surfaced even in the 1990s, despite being off the air for more than a quarter-century. In March 1993, the "Bulletin Board" column of the *Saint Paul Pioneer Press* printed a reader's request for a picture of Axel. The columnist confessed that the *Pioneer Press* library did not have a single picture of the old Scandihoovian, but the paper did run a publicity still of Clellan from 1941. That was enough to trigger an avalanche of Axel anecdotes and Birdies from readers that lasted more than a week.

One of the works on exhibit in the Arts Building at the Minnesota State Fair in 1995 was a pen-and-ink collage drawing by artist Marc Johnson entitled *Ink Heads, Part 1*. Included in the illustration, among more than 170 images of various pop culture icons from Vincent Price to The Beatles, was one Axel Torgeson. The following year, the State Fair was the setting for the crime caper *The Mortal Nuts* by Minneapolis novelist Pete Hautman. The main character, the no-nonsense owner of a taco stand at the Fair, was named Axel; another, a substance-abusing floozy who unwittingly sets in motion a murderous chain of events, was called Carmen. However, Pete noted wryly, "I left Towser out of it."

Detail of *Ink Heads, Part 1* by Marc Johnson

In 1995, Twin Cities public television station KTCA-TV (later TPT-TV) released a sequel to *Lost Twin Cities*, the most successful program that the station had ever produced. Like its predecessor, *Lost Twin Cities II* was narrated by Dave Moore, and the climax of the special – as well as the focus of most of the promotion for the program – was a segment about *Axel and His Dog*. Featuring interviews with Don Stolz, Mary Davies, and others, as

How's your boyfriend – Harry?

well as numerous Axel film clips, the segment set off a new wave of Axelmania and *Lost Twin Cities II* was another winner for KTCA.

Ron Peluso, a director at the Great American History Theatre in Saint Paul, happened to watch *Lost Twin Cities II* and was charmed by Axel, whom he had not seen before. He contacted Don Stolz and asked him to write a play about the old TV show that he'd done with Clellan. In October 1998, the play *Axel and His Dog* premiered at the Great American History Theatre. It was a comical and captivating look at the early days of local television, as well as a touching testament to Don and Clellan's friendship.

The play was directed by Peluso and starred Steve Shaffer as Clellan Card and Axel, Sue Scott as Mary Davies and Carmen the Nurse, and Don's son Tom Stolz as Don, Towser, and Tallulah. The first run of the play was so successful, it was remounted at the Old Log Theater with most of the original cast during the summer of 1999. *Axel and His Dog* was also revived at the Great American History Theatre in 2003.

Across the country, baby boomers still recall their own local children's programs with great affection. And like many other things, old TV shows have been granted a second life on the internet. Dozens of websites are devoted to various local kidvid programs, and sometimes they pop up in unexpected places. Steve Almaas, bass player of the seminal Twin Cities punk-rock band The Suicide Commandos, prominently lists his "Influences" on his MySpace page, including (among others) The Beatles, Patti Smith, Billie Holiday, and Clellan Card.

Decades after his final broadcast from the tree house, Axel lives on in the hearts of the people who grew up watching him. Memories of his endearing idiocy even inspired one fan to write a book telling the whole story of a television show called *Axel and His Dog*, and a funny, charming, simply marvelous gentleman named Clellan Covey Card.

ACKNOWLEDGMENTS

WRITING THIS BOOK has been a great experience, and I couldn't have done it without the aid of a great many people. First and foremost, I wish to thank Michael S. Card, Clellan's son. He has given this project his enthusiastic support from the very beginning, and helped me in myriad ways. Without him, this book would not exist.

I also especially want to thank Don Stolz, Harry Jones, and Mary Davies. Along with Clellan Card, they were the creators of the *Axel and His Dog* television show. They submitted to numerous interviews with me without complaint, and did their best to answer all my questions.

I'm indebted to WCCO-TV, particularly former station manager Ken Rees and producer Ron Hinze. A special vote of thanks to film editor Claude Heisch, not only for his many kindnesses, but also for his crucial role in preserving the Axel films.

Many of Clellan's other co-workers and fellow broadcasters shared their memories with me or assisted me in other ways, and I'm very grateful to them all: Frank Butler, Tom Cousins, Northrop "Bun" Dawson, Jr., Glenn Devery, Bill Dietrichson, Roger Erickson, Ernie Garven, Wally Green, Mel Jass, Rodger Kent, Bud Kraehling, Joyce Lamont, Daryl Laub, Allan Lotsberg, Perry Martin, Dave Moore, Ken Pack, Jeanne Arland Peterson, Don Pottratz, John Sieberz, Dick Stuck, Mel Tollefson, Jimmy Valentine, and Stan Wolfson.

I also would like to extend my thanks to WCCO-AM radio, and especially Paul Bergly, as well as Tom Gavaras, Laura Lee Geraghty, Ben Johnston, and Jerry Miller. Many thanks, too, to KSTP-AM radio, in particular Connie Eckart, Eric Doherty, Dixie Hansen, and Ryan Barnholdt.

I would particularly like to thank William F. Lund for making available many rare radio recordings, and for sharing his knowledge about Twin Cities broadcasting history with me. Others who generously provided me with unique radio and television recordings include Kathleen Abel, Richard W. Bann, Lou Bohl, Ernie Garven, Mike Merrick, Patrick Sweeney, Tracy Tolzmann, Robert and Jim Wild, and Dennis Wilfahrt.

I want to extend my gratitude to the Pavek Museum of Broadcasting, particularly director Steve Raymer and staffer Tom Mittelstaedt, for their assistance. I also spent many enjoyable hours immersed in research at the History Center of the Minnesota Historical Society, where I found a wealth of data and enjoyed the benefits of its helpful and capable staff. Other archives and people that were helpful include the Blake School and Caren Aronson and Sarah Carroll; the Excelsior Historical Society and Betty Peck; St. Margaret's Academy and Sister Mary Kraft; St. Thomas Academy; the University of St. Thomas; the Walter and Wilson Libraries at the University of Minnesota; the George Sverdrup Library at Augsburg College; and the Special Collections Department of the Minneapolis Public Library.

A big "Thank you!" to Minnesnowtan Louie Anderson for his warm and funny foreword. Noel Holston, formerly of the *Minneapolis Star Tribune*, was enormously helpful and encouraging; I can't thank him enough. Dan Kelly and Linda James of the *Saint Paul Pioneer Press* also gave me assistance. I'm very grateful to Julie Moden Enroth and Carol Schaubach, the founders of the Axel and Carmen Fan Club, who gave me much information about the last years of Axel's show, as well as a ton of memorabilia and audio recordings of the TV show. I'd also particularly like to thank Terry Fisk, who shared the fruits of his research into Twin Cities children's television, including recordings of interviews that he did in the 1980s. Kristian Berg and Mark J. Hinsted kindly sent me copies of interviews that they had conducted as well.

Elaine Hogan, a close friend of Marion's and Clellan's since high school, was an invaluable source of information about Clellan's family and the early years. Clellan's relatives William Card, Marilyn Brock, and Maury Crowley told me about the Card and Satterlee clans. Merrill Madsen, Stanley Tull, and Jerry Walsh reminisced about their friend Peter Card; Jim Lavin, Chuck Stanek, and Tom Welch did likewise about their pal John Card. Family friend Noel Allard contributed a number of anecdotes as well. Clellan L. Card helped me discover the source of Clellan C. Card's name. Dennis Blenis gave me insight into what Clellan's final year was like. Clellan's physicians, Dr. A. Boyd Thomes and Dr. James L. McKenna, reviewed the extant medical records and critiqued the relevant portions of the manuscript, for which I'm very grateful.

During this project, I've had the aid and support of many coworkers and friends at Greatapes Corporation, the College of Comic Book Knowledge, the Nostalgia Zone, and the Block-Heads Tent of the Sons of the Desert. In particular, I want to mention Curt Almsted, Paul Brennecke, Chris Büdel, Dave Coscio, Pat Devine, John Flomer, Jim Foster, Ralph Johnson, Steve Jones, Tracy Tolzmann, Joe Walker, and Jim and Diane Woelm. Thanks to fellow Block-Head Arnie Fogel for his identification of *Axel and His Dog*'s first theme song. I especially want to single out Steve Kent and Neil Sontag for their assistance in assembling the DVD which accompanies this book.

I'm also indebted to a legion of collectors, dealers, scroungers, and scavengers who dug up rare Clellan Card and Axel artifacts for me (keep looking, gang!): Jon Anderson, Kent Hazen, Byron and Brian Hendrickson, Tom Karason, Corey "Ed" Lindquist, Jan Lorsung, Cindy Mainella, Dave Mruz, Joel Rasmussen, Steve Schoneck, Ron Smisek, Clint Tucker, Arvid Wallin, and the Axel hunter *extraordinaire*, Bob Peterson.

Jennifer Manion, my editor at Beaver's Pond Press, and proofreader Michele Bassett made this a better book than it otherwise would be. Thanks to Pam Scheunemann, Chris Long, and Kelly Doudna of Mighty Media for the book design, and to Milt Adams and Dara Moore of Beaver's Pond for seeing the project through. I'm also grateful to Ann Regan, editor of the Minnesota Historical Society Press, for her input. My friends Michael Rosen, Jerry Modjeski, and Paul Bergly gave me detailed critiques of the manuscript as well. I'm grateful to artist Marc Johnson for the use of his Axel illustration, and for all his other help. I also very much appreciate the support and encouragement I got from Billy Ingram, author and editor of *TVParty! Television's Untold Tales* and webmaster of TVParty.com.

Many other people also helped me in a variety of ways: Bill Aberman, Wayne Adams, Biddy Bastien, Michael Beard, Bob Benham, Gail

Bisch, Laura Boyce, Cathie Briggs, Judy Bryson, Marilyn Cathcart, Alice Cavanaugh, Don Cavitt, Amy Claussen and the Huber Funeral Home, Chris Colestock, Roy Dobie, Barbara Economon, Patricia Feeley, Connie French, Bernie Gaytko, John Gehring, Barbara Gibelyou, Dominic and Frances Giovanelli, Corey Gordon, Norma Keeney Gordon, Mary Griffin, Irene Hagen, Ron Hall, Boyd Hanson, Marian Haugesag, Pete Hautman, Tim Hollis, Don Holm, Bob Jackson, Beulah Jahr, Jeff Jewell, Scott Johnson, Jo Jones, Paul Joyce, Charlie Kaiser, Dan Kaster, Alice Kavanagh, Jack Kennelly, Daryl Kruder, Bev Larson, Val Larson, Sharon Lee, Darel Leipold, Marvin Levoir, Connie Lindberg, Rod Lord, Jim Marazzo, Stu Mathews, Al Mayer, Maryann McKenna, Bill Metchnik, Jim Monitor, Verne Palmberg, Dan Peterson, Bob Pratt, Wallace Pratt, David Prin, Ellen Prin, John Prin, Tom Prin, Jim Proft, Pat Proft, Clayton Radue, Dennis Rafftery, Carol Ramberg, Frankie Roberts, Mary Severson, Kris Sexton and the Minneapolis Aquatennial Association, Marilyn Sherf, Ruby Starr, Art Steffes, Larry Stelter, Tom Stolz, Dick Stuck, Marty Theis, Harley Toberman, Vern Tukua, Judith Wanhala, the Werness Brothers Chapel, Ken Witt, James Wold, Dick Wolf, and Henry J. Wudlick. I thank them all, and I hope they'll buy the book now that their names are in it.

A special thanks to my late parents, Jane and Kent Westley, for all their advice and encouragement. And many, many thanks to Rebecca Scott, too, for everything.

Last but certainly not least, I'd like to thank my friend, Mitch Griffin, who inadvertently set this whole thing in motion when he gave me a videotape of the Channel 2 show *Kids' TV Nostalgia Hour*. It's all his fault!

SELECTED BIBLIOGRAPHY

Books

Aden, Bob. *The Way It Was* (Excelsior, MN: The Old Log Theater, 1989).

Barnouw, Erik. *A Tower in Babel: A History of Broadcasting in the United States, Volume I* (New York: Oxford University Press, 1966).

Barnouw, Erik. *The Golden Web: A History of Broadcasting in the United States, Volume II* (New York: Oxford University Press, 1968).

Barnouw, Erik. *The Image Empire: A History of Broadcasting in the United States, Volume III* (New York: Oxford University Press, 1970).

Cantril, Hadley and Gordon Allport. *The Psychology of Radio* (New York: Harper, 1935).

Connah, Douglas Duff. *How to Build the Radio Audience* (New York: Harper and Brothers, 1938).

Cornelius, Chase, editor. *One Hundred Years of Trust, 1884–1984* (Minneapolis: Northrup, King & Co., 1984).

Crews, Albert. *Radio Production Directing* (Cambridge, MA: Houghton Mifflin Co., 1944).

Davis, Stephen. *Say Kids! What Time Is It?* (Boston: Little, Brown & Co., 1987).

DeHaven, Bob. *55 Years Before the Mike* (Minneapolis: James D. Thueson, 1985).

Dunning, John. *Tune In Yesterday* (Englewood Cliffs, NJ: Prentice-Hall, Inc., 1976).

Fischer, Stuart. *Kids' TV: The First 25 Years* (New York: Facts on File, 1983).

Grossman, Gary H. *Saturday Morning TV* (New York: Arlington House, 1987 edition).

Hardman, Benedict E. *Everybody Called Him Cedric* (St. Paul: Twin City Federal, 1970).

Hollis, Tim. *Cousin Cliff: 40 Magical Years in Television* (Birmingham, AL: Campbell's Publishing, 1991).

Hollis, Tim. *Hi There, Boys and Girls! America's Local Children's TV Programs* (Jackson, MS: University Press of Mississippi, 2001).

Ingersoll, Charles W. *Minnesota Airwaves 1912 Through 1939 and Radio Trivia* (Cloquet, MN: Northern Printery, undated).

Ingram, Billy, editor/author. *TV Party! Television's Untold Tales* (Chicago & Los Angeles: Bonus Books, 2002).

Lewis, Tom. *Empire of the Air: The Men Who Made Radio* (New York: Harper Collins, 1991).

MacDonald, J. Fred. *Don't Touch That Dial! Radio Programming in American Life from 1920 to 1960* (Chicago: Nelson-Hall, 1979 (1991 reprint)).

Maltin, Leonard and Richard W. Bann. *Our Gang: The Life and Times of the Little Rascals* (New York: Crown Publishers, 1977).

Meyer, Ellen W., et al. *A Picture Book of the Excelsior Amusement Park ... from Rise to Demise 1924–1974* (Excelsior, MN: Excelsior-Lake Minnetonka Historical Society, 1991).

Millett, Larry. *Lost Twin Cities* (St. Paul: Minnesota Historical Society Press, 1992).

Sarjeant, Charles F., editor. *The First Forty: WCCO Radio* (Minneapolis: WCCO Radio/T.S. Denison & Co., 1964).

Smith, Buffalo Bob and Donna McCrohan. *Howdy and Me: Buffalo Bob's Own Story* (New York: Plume, 1990).

Williams, Bob and Chuck Hartley. *Good Neighbor to the Northwest 1924–1974* (Minneapolis: WCCO Radio, 1974).

Periodicals

Adams, Cedric. "In This Corner" column, *Minneapolis Star*, 1935–1961.

Adams, Cedric. "The Morning Mirthquake," *Movie and Radio Guide*, July 1940.

Beck, Joe. "Pioneering in Television in the Twin Cities," *Minnesota History*, Fall 1979 (46/7).

Card, Clellan. "One Man's Opinion" column, *Minnetonka Record*, summer 1962.

Jones, Will. "After Last Night" column, *Minneapolis Tribune*, 1954–1975.

Levitan, Sam. "That Card Party," *Northwest Life* magazine, Vol. 18 #2, February 1945.

Ryan, Howard. "Axel – He's a Card," *St. Paul Pioneer Press*, 21 April 1957, *TV Tab* magazine.

"Axel and His Dog," *Variety*, 11 August 1954.

Newsletters

The Seed Bag (Northrup, King & Company, 1936–1944).

Telepulse (television ratings, 1954–1961).

Tree House Tribune (WCCO-TV/Axel and Carmen Fan Club, 1965–1966).

Views from Channel 4 (WCCO-TV, 1954–1962).

Booklets, Pamphlets, etc.

Leipold, Darel and LaVerna. *The Excelsior Amusement Park "Those Were the Days"* (Leipold's of Excelsior, 1991).

Stanville, Martha and Devery, Glenn. *A Score for 4: 1949–1969* (WCCO-TV, 1969).

Clellan Card's Laugh Book (Northrup, King & Co., 1940).

Cracks by Card (Marshall-Wells, 1949).

A Day Behind the Dial with WCCO (WCCO radio, circa 1939).

Inside WCCO Television 1949–1974 (WCCO-TV, 1974).

It Doesn't Make Sense – SRO (Standing Room Only) at 7 AM promotional flyer, (Olmsted-Hewitt Inc., May 1939).

A Party Comes to Life AT DAWN promotional flyer, (WCCO radio/Olmsted-Hewitt Inc., May 1939).

Saturday Morning Open House Recipes (WCCO radio, 1942).

Since 1949 (WCCO-TV, 1979).

WCCO: For 30 Years Good Neighbor to the Northwest (WCCO radio, 1954).

WCCO Radio – The Northwest's 50,000-Watt Giant (WCCO radio, circa 1957).

WCCO – Service to the Northwest (WCCO radio, circa 1930).

Audio-Visual Media

The 30th Anniversary of WCCO Radio radio program (WCCO radio, October 1954).

Axel television programs (WCCO-TV, June 1962; audio only: December 1964–March 1965).

Axel and His Dog television programs (WCCO-TV, 1955–1957; audio only: December 1958).

Axel and Carmen: "Axel's Famous Version of 'The Night Before Christmas'" b/w Clancy the Cop and Willie Ketchem: "Close Call for Santa" phonograph record (WCCO-TV, 1964).

Axel "Goodie Reel" (WCCO-TV out-takes, compiled circa August 1956).

Carmen television programs (WCCO-TV, 1 July 1974 and 25 March 1977).

Casey's Comedy Album for Kids phonograph record (Sound 80, 1973).

Clancy and Willie television programs (WCCO-TV, circa 1968, 1 July 1974, and 25 March 1977).

Clellan Card's Humor television program (WCCO-TV, 20 September 1976).

"Clellan Card's Notebook" personal tape recordings, undated (circa late 1950s).

Country Holiday television program (WCCO-TV, 29 December 1954).

Dunking at the Card Table radio programs (KSTP radio, 1 November 1945 & 30 January 1946).

Flame Room Coffee Time radio programs (WCCO radio, January 1950).

Kids' TV Nostalgia Hour television program (KTCA-TV, 1987).

Kingscrost Lecture transcription disk (Northrup, King & Co., circa December 1941).

Lost Twin Cities II television program (KTCA-TV, 1995).

Lunch with Casey television programs (WTCN-TV, circa 1965–1972).

Miscellany

Card, Clellan. "The Night Before Christmas, a Parody Done in Swedish Dialect by Clellan Card on the Northrup, King & Co.'s Christmas Program, December 23, 1938" written transcription (Northrup, King & Co., c. 1938).

Cavanor, Hayle C. memo to Mr. [Carl] Burkland, 25 October 1938.

Godt, Gene, compiler. "Axel Day" scrapbook (WCCO-TV, 1957).

Haines, Jerry. "History of Radio Station WDGY" (University of Minnesota master's thesis, 1970).

Moden, Julie, compiler. "The Axel and Carmen Fan Club" scrapbook (1965–1966).

Moden, Julie. "History of the Axel and Carmen Fan Club" (unpublished manuscript, circa 1966).

Pufall, Michael Erwin. "A History of the Old Log Theater in Greenwood, Minnesota 1940–1970" (University of Minnesota dissertation, 1974).

Thomes, Dr. A. Boyd. "Personal History – Card, Mr. Clelland [sic] C." (Abbott Hospital, 29 March 1965).

Aquatennial folders (Minneapolis Library, 1940–1950).

Excelsior Amusement Park scrapbooks (1930s–1960s).

Author Interviews

Bill Aberman (September 1995), Noel Allard (May 1995), Bob Benham (March 1994), Gail Bisch (1993), Dennis Blenis (June and July 1997), Judy Bryson (May 1993), Clellan Locke Card (June 1997), Michael S. Card (February 1993), William Card (March 1997), Chris Colestock (March 1994), Tom Cousins (February 1994, October 1995, and March 1996), Maurice Crowley (November 1994 and June 1997), Northrop "Bun" Dawson, Jr. (April 1993), Glenn Devery (March 1994), Bill Dietrichson (December 1992), Julie Moden Enroth (March 1994), Roger Erickson (October 1995), Ernie Garven (April 1994 and April 1995), Corey Gordon (June 1997), Wally Green (July 1996), Boyd Hanson (March 1996), Pete Hautman (July 1996), Elaine Hogan (December 1992 and October 1993), Beulah Jahr (March 1993), Mel Jass (October 1995 and November 1995), Scott Johnson (May 1996), Harry Jones (December 1992, August 1995, and January 1997), Jo Jones (December 1992), Dan Kaster (March 1994), Rodger Kent (June 1997), Daryl Laub (June 1997), Jim Lavin (May 1997), Marvin Levoir (March 1994), Allan Lotsberg (November 1993), Merrill Madsen (March 1994), Perry Martin (December 1995), Dr. James L. McKenna (May 1997), Maryann McKenna (May 1997), Dave Moore (March 1994), Mary Davies Orfield (December 1992 and June 1997), Ken Pack (August 1997), Jeanne Arland Peterson (April 1994), Don Pottratz (May 1993), David and John Prin (March 1994), Ellen Prin

(March 1994), Frankie Roberts (January 1997), Carol Schaubach (March 1994), John Sieberz (July 1996), Chuck Stanek (May 1997), Art Steffes (July 1997), Don Stolz (January 1993, October 1994, and January 1997), Dick Stuck (May 1993), Dr. A. Boyd Thomes (March 1997), Mel Tollefson (October 1995), Stanley Tull (April 1993), Jimmy Valentine (July and August 1996), Jerry Walsh (March 1994), Tom Welch (May 1997), Dennis Wilfahrt (April 1993 and August 1996), Stan Wolfson (March 1993).

NOTES

INTRODUCTION: "HI, KIDS! DISS ISS AXEL!"

AUTHOR INTERVIEWS
Michael Card.

MISCELLANY
Michael Card, family genealogy.
"This is Axel ..." WCCO-TV ad (quoting ARBitron ratings data from May 1957), *Sponsor* magazine, July 1957.
Untitled typescript promotional document (WCCO radio, circa 1939).

CHAPTER 1: CLELLY

FOOTNOTES

1   In fact, William Card was a bit younger than anyone at the university may have realized. His University of Minnesota transcript gives his date of birth as May 5, 1878, rather than the correct date of November 24. At graduation, he would have appeared to be twenty years old instead of his true age of nineteen. The transcript also notes that his diploma was withheld until his twenty-first birthday, which perhaps explains the discrepancy. Since William had completed all the necessary coursework, the delay may have been due to some sort of minimum age requirement. The dentist-in-waiting may have fudged his date of birth in order to get his diploma a little sooner.

2   Over the years, Clellan saw his unique first name garbled with galling frequency. It was often misspelled "Clelland," sometimes "Clellen" or "Cleland," and occasionally even "Cullen," or "Clullen." His local fame was no insurance against such indignities – it merely provided more opportunities to mangle his moniker. When he starred in the very first Twin Cities color telecast, his own TV station called him "Clelland" Card in the credits. And after more than thirty years as a fixture on local radio and television, his front-page obituary in one Minneapolis paper contained the same mistake. Examples include "Sixty Pupils Billed to Perform Tonight," *Minneapolis Morning Tribune*, 5 May 1916, p. 5; D.A.W., "Off a Reporter's Cuff" column, *Minneapolis Journal*, 27 December 1935, p. 17; "Cleland [*sic*] Card to Free-Lance," *Billboard*, 4 November 1944, p. 11; "Clelland [*sic*] and Dad Card Will Be School Guests," *Minneapolis Star*, 31 October 1949, p. 24; "Clelland [*sic*] Card Dies at 62," *Minneapolis Star*, 13 April 1966, p. 1; *Kids' TV Nostalgia Hour*, KTCA-TV, 1987 (end credits).

AUTHOR INTERVIEWS
Clellan Locke Card, Michael Card, Elaine Hogan, Jimmy Valentine.

BOOKS
Louise Ayers Garnett, *Master Will of Stratford* (New York: MacMillan, 1916).
Russell L. Olson, *The Electric Railways of Minnesota.* (Hopkins, MN: Minnesota Transportation Museum, 1976).
Marion Daniel Shutter, *History of Minneapolis, Gateway to the Northwest* (Chicago-Minneapolis: S.J. Clarke Publishing Company, 1923).
Elsdon C. Smith, *New Dictionary of American Family Names* (New York: Harper & Row, 1973).

PERIODICALS
Card, "One Man's Opinion" column, *Minnetonka Record*, 7 June and 16 August 1962.
Levitan, art. cit.
"Clelland [*sic*] and Dad Card Will Be School Guests," art. cit.
"Dr. Card, Pioneer Dentist, Dies," *Minneapolis Star*, 1 June 1950.
"In Social Circles," *The Minneapolis Journal*, 30 May 1901.
"Shakespeare as Boy of Twelve Shown by Pupils," *Minneapolis Morning Tribune*, 6 May 1916.
"Sixty Pupils Billed to Perform Tonight," art. cit.

AUDIO-VISUAL MEDIA
Axel and His Dog television program, 31 July 1955.
Various Card family photographs and home movies.

CORRESPONDENCE
William H. Card, letter to Mary Card, 13 October 1949.

MISCELLANY
Michael Card, family genealogy.
William H. Card, household ledger, May 1901–November 1906.
"In Memoriam," *M.A.C. Gopher*, July 1950 (Volume 35).
Minneapolis City Directory, 1892–1906.
William Henry [*sic*] Card transcript, University of Minnesota College of Dentistry.

CHAPTER 2: AMONG THE ROSEBUDS AND CACTUS

FOOTNOTES
3 The meaning of Clellan's enigmatic title is uncertain, but the "rosebuds" may symbolize the students and the "cactus" may be the schoolteacher. The final line, "To grant an early car," undoubtedly means permitting the student to take a trolley car home from school at an earlier than usual time.

AUTHOR INTERVIEWS
Michael Card.

BOOKS
Shutter, op. cit.

PERIODICALS

Card, "One Man's Opinion" column, *Minnetonka Record*, 16 August 1962.

The *Blake Torch* (Blake School newspaper), 1918–1922, *passim*.

Isaac Card obituary, *Minneapolis Morning Tribune*, 2 September 1918.

AUDIO-VISUAL MEDIA

Various Card family photographs.

CORRESPONDENCE

Clellan Card, letters to William H. Card, 14 October & 24 October 1923.

[Blake headmaster Raymond B. Johnson], unsigned copies of letters to Dr. W. H. Card, 1920–1922.

G.W. Marque Maier, letter to Mr. Newton, 12 August 1918.

MISCELLANY

Clellan C. Card diploma, West High School, 14 June 1923.

Michael Card, family genealogy.

The *Callopan* (Blake School yearbook), 1919, 1920, 1921, 1922.

The *Hesperian* (West High School yearbook), 1918 (Volume X), 1923 (Volume XV).

CHAPTER 3: MARRYIN' MARION AND OTHER ENGAGEMENTS

FOOTNOTES

4   The erroneous claim appears in: an untitled typescript promotional document (WCCO radio, circa 1939), p. 1; *Clellan Card's Laugh Book* (Northrup, King & Co, 1940), p. 3; *Just a Yawn at Dawn* booklet (Northrup, King & Co., circa 1943), p. 2; *Cracks by Card* joke book, (Marshall-Wells stores/WCCO radio; summer 1949), p.4; *Axel's Joke Book*, WCCO-TV, 1956, p. 15. Interviews wherein Clellan says only that he attended college: Levitan, "Card Party," p. 20 (which specifies that he did not get a diploma); "Town Toppers" column, *Minneapolis Star*, Thursday 6 February 1958, p. 4; [Moden], "Axel: Clellan Card," *Tree House Tribune*, May 1965 (Vol. I, #4), p. 4.

AUTHOR INTERVIEWS

Michael Card, Maurice Crowley, Elaine Hogan.

BOOKS

Barnouw, *A Tower in Babel*.

PERIODICALS

Levitan, art. cit.

The *Blake Torch*, April 1926.

"Clellan Covey Card and Marion Jean Satterlee Wed in St. Thomas Church," *Minneapolis Journal*, 10 October 1928.

"Miss Satterlee Weds Clellan Covey Card at St. Thomas Church," *Minneapolis Star*, 10 October 1928.

NEWSLETTERS

[Moden], art. cit.

AUDIO-VISUAL MEDIA

Axel and His Dog television program, 11 March 1956.

Various Card family photographs and home movies.

CORRESPONDENCE
Clellan Card, letters to family members, 1923–1925.
Zarine T. Dotivala (Rutgers University Associate Registrar), letter to the author, February 1997.
Newspaper article included with letter, circa February 1924.

MISCELLANY
Clellan Card transcript, University of Minnesota, 1924.
Dayesye (St. Margaret's Academy yearbook), 1923.
Minneapolis City Directory, 1926–1932.
The Scarlet Letter (Rutgers yearbook), 1924.
Untitled typescript promotional document (WCCO radio, circa 1939).

CHAPTER 4: DIPPING INTO THE AIRWAVES

AUTHOR INTERVIEWS
Ernie Garven.

INTERVIEWS BY OTHERS
Marion Card, conducted by Bob DeHaven (Minneapolis Public Library, 1976).

BOOKS
Barnouw, *A Tower in Babel.*
Cornelius, ed., op. cit.
DeHaven, op. cit.
Ingersoll, op. cit.
Lewis, op. cit.
Sarjeant, ed., op. cit.

PERIODICALS
Adams, "In This Corner" column, *Minneapolis Star*, 1 December 1935.
Adams, "The Morning Mirthquake," art. cit.
Levitan, art. cit.
Forrest Powers, "TV-Radio Chatter" column, *Minneapolis Star*, 25 March 1960.
D.A.W., "Off a Reporter's Cuff," column, *Minneapolis Journal*, 27 December 1935.
"8,000 Show Visitors See Television," *Minneapolis Tribune*, 30 September 1930.
"100,000 to See Radio Exhibits, Manager Says," *Minneapolis Star*, 30 September 1930.
"Came the Dawn at WCCO," *Minneapolis Journal* Variety section, 6 December 1936.
"Dealers Parade in Loop; Television Tests Special Feature at Auditorium," *Minneapolis Star*, 29 September 1930.
"First Television to Be Sent Here," *Minneapolis Journal*, 24 September 1930.
"From the Production Centres," *Variety*, 27 October 1954.
Special Radio section, *Minneapolis Journal*, 28 September 1930.
"Television Set Ready for Show," *Minneapolis Journal*, 25 September 1930.
"Television to Be Displayed Here at Radio Show," *Minneapolis Star*, 24 September 1930.
"Town Toppers" column, *Minneapolis Star*, 6 February 1958.
"University's Night to End Radio Show," *Minneapolis Journal*, 4 October 1930.
WCCO radio ads, *Minneapolis Tribune*, January, April, and September 1936.

NEWSLETTERS

[Moden], art. cit.

Rome A. Riebeth, "Northrup-King's Interesting Broadcasts Attract a Big Audience," *Seed World*, 21 April 1939.

"Do You Listen to Pop?" *The Seed Bag*, 14 October 1936 (V36, #14).

"Flowers for Card from Edison High," *The Seed Bag*, 8 March 1940 (V44, #10).

"From Our Radio Fans" column (Victoria Nelson letter), *The Seed Bag*, 22 December 1936 (V36, #20).

"Of Interest to All Northrup-King Folks," *The Seed Bag*, 24 August 1939 (V43, #10).

BOOKLETS, PAMPHLETS, ETC.

Clellan Card's Laugh Book, op. cit.

Cracks by Card, op. cit.

It Doesn't Make Sense, op. cit.

WCCO – Service to the Northwest, op. cit.

AUDIO-VISUAL MEDIA

Dunking at the Card Table, rec. cit.

CORRESPONDENCE

Cavanor, memo. cit.

MISCELLANY

Michael Card, family genealogy.

Haines, op. cit.

"Clellan Card – The One Clown, Multivoiced Show" postcard (Northrup, King & Co., postmarked February 1937).

"The Hormel Chili Beaners!" grocery store display (Hormel, undated).

Minneapolis City Directory, 1932–1935.

"Presenting – Clellan Card – A Salesman for Fels Naphtha," typescript promotional document, (WCCO radio, circa April 1940).

Untitled typescript promotional document (WCCO radio, circa 1939).

CHAPTER 5: AXEL AND HIS ... HOG?

FOOTNOTES

5   Bob DeHaven, in his 1985 book *55 Years Before the Mike*, rather incoherently claimed that "Some of [Clellan's] act was done in a genuine Swedish accent, not the bogus vaude-ville accent, he learned from an uncle." This is incorrect and it is also odd, because DeHaven himself conducted the 1976 interview with Marion Card – Clellan's wife for nearly thirty-eight years – wherein she told the story of the Swedish housekeeper.

6   A photo at the bottom of page 19 of *The First Forty: The Story of WCCO Radio*, and reproduced on page 50 of this book, might depict a broadcast of *Axel the Newscaster*. The program is not named in the photo caption but it was broadcast in the 1930s, featured "news of the day," and both Clellan and Max Karl participated. *Axel the Newscaster* fits all these criteria.

7   A slide presentation has been inferred from the bell tones that periodically occur on the disk. These probably indicate points where the operator of the projector is supposed to advance to the next slide. In addition, some of Axel's comments refer specifically to Clellan's appearance, which would make no sense unless pictures were being shown.

More evidence can be found in a brief note in the Northrup, King newsletter, *The Seed Bag*, of November 21, 1941, which mentions a Clellan Card photo session for the Corn Department. Although the reason for the photo shoot is not specified, the date and the department make it very likely that the photo session was for the "Kingscrost Lecture" presentation. Unfortunately, the slides or photos apparently have been lost.

INTERVIEWS BY OTHERS

Marion Card, int. cit.

BOOKS

Cantril and Allport, op. cit.

Connah, op. cit.

MacDonald, op. cit.

PERIODICALS

Axel the Newscaster WCCO radio ad, *Minneapolis Star*, 17 February 1937.

AUDIO-VISUAL MEDIA

"Kingscrost Lecture," rec. cit.

CORRESPONDENCE

Cavanor, memo. cit.

MISCELLANY

Untitled typescript promotional document (WCCO radio, circa 1939).

CHAPTER 6: THE MORNING MIRTHQUAKE

FOOTNOTES

8   *The First Forty: The Story of WCCO Radio* (Charles F. Sarjeant, editor; WCCO radio/ T.S. Denison & Co., 1964) claims that Clellan "aired his classic version every Christmas from 1934 to 1963" (p. 19). This is incorrect. There is no evidence whatsoever that Clellan did the parody before 1938. The notion that this tradition began in 1934 was probably based on the fact that Clellan was hired by WCCO radio that year. However, he didn't have a program of his own until 1936, so it seems unlikely that he would have had the opportunity to perform the piece before then. Furthermore, *none* of the many letters in Northrup, King's company newsletter which comment on the 1937 Christmas program mention Clellan performing "The Night Before Christmas" ("From Our Radio Fans." *The Seed Bag*, 31 December 1937 (V38, #22), p. 5; *The Seed Bag*, 7 January 1938 (V39, #1), p. 6.). Yet the following year, the parody was published in *The Seed Bag* shortly after Christmas (3 January 1939 (V42, #1), p. 10–11) and issued on "parchment" to satisfy hundreds of requests for copies, indicating the tremendous response it had elicited. If Clellan had recited it in 1937, it seems very odd that no one mentioned it.

Good Neighbor to the Northwest 1924–1974 (Bob Williams and Chuck Hartley, WCCO radio, 1974) also claims that Clellan did the parody every year from 1934 to 1963 (p. 89). This information was evidently derived directly from *The First Forty*, which was published in 1964. However, when *The First Forty* went to press, Clellan would not have given that year's performance of "The Night Before Christmas" by then, and of course the book could not cite a performance that had not yet occurred. Clellan definitely *did* perform the parody in 1964; in fact, a recording of it was released by WCCO-TV that year (see also Diane Mills, "What's for Yule Viewing Locally?" which describes Axel and Carmen's upcoming "special Christmas show which was written and produced by Carmen. Axel will read his famous version of 'The Night Before Christmas' and more Yuletide fun is promised." (*TV Times*, 19–25 December 1964 (Vol. 5 #32), p. 4)). Clellan was still appearing on television during the 1965 Christmas season as well, so it was probably in that year that he recited the poem for the final time. Therefore, it is most likely that Clellan Card performed "The Night Before Christmas" from 1938 to 1965, a total of twenty-eight years.

9   Clellan tinkered with the parody a bit over the years. Another version, dating from 1958, differs somewhat from the 1938 transcription, and the recording from 1964 has additional differences. For example, the "little shavers" of 1938 have become "little stinkers" in 1958, and by 1964 they are "little monsters." After 1944, the lawn was no longer a "Northrup, King" one. In 1958, the animals pulling Santa's sleigh are "eight great big rain-horses," but by 1964, they have shrunk back into "teensy-weensy reinhorses." In the litany of names, the superfluous "On Pittsburg" was dropped early on, and by the 1960s "On, Cosmetics!" had turned into "On, Tackhead!" Although Santa is called fat in later versions, he's not compared to an old hog. His belly also stopped shaking "like a bottle of likker" when he snickered; it shook like the more kid-friendly "home yiggley yelly." By the 1950s, when Santa gives a whistle to his team, it isn't also described as one "he had promised them for Christmas." And in the later versions, the phrase "Ay hope yu get vat yu vant" has been replaced by the original poem's closing words: "Good night!"

AUTHOR INTERVIEWS
Gail Bisch, David Prin, John Prin.

BOOKS
Sarjeant, ed., op. cit.

PERIODICALS
Adams, "In This Corner" column, *Minneapolis Star*, 12 April and 16 April 1938.
Adams, "The Morning Mirthquake," art. cit.
Herman Land, "The Storz Bombshell," *Television*, May 1957.
"*Baseball Resumé*," WCCO radio ad, *Minneapolis Star*, 19 August 1938.
"Card Announces Baseball Game," WCCO radio ad, *Minneapolis Star*, 6 May 1938.
"Card Co-Host of *The Extra Inning*," WCCO radio ad, *Minneapolis Star*, 13 May 1938.
"Heads Program," *Minneapolis Star*, 1 April 1937.
"The New Home of WCCO," *Minneapolis Star*, 9 April 1938, special section.
"On *Meet the Missus*," *Minneapolis Star*, 21 May 1937.
"Planes, Bombs, Chimes to Honor WCCO Studio," *Minneapolis Star*, 6 April 1938.
"*Sportsman's Special*," WCCO radio ad, *Minneapolis Star*, 5 February 1938, Variety section.
"Toby Prin," *Twin Cities Tele-Viewer*, 14–31 May 1950 (Vol. 1, #2).
"WCCO Dedicates New Studios Tonight," *Minneapolis Star*, 7 April 1938.
"WCCO Has a 'Housewarming'," *Minneapolis Star*, 8 April 1938.

NEWSLETTERS
Riebeth, art. cit.
"150 Visitors to WCCO Studio in Past Week or Two," *The Seed Bag*, 11 February 1938 (V39, #4).
"April First Radio Show," *The Seed Bag*, 7 April 1939 (V42, #14).
"April Fools' Show," *Tidings*, 15 April 1939.
"Big April First Radio Show," *The Seed Bag*, 3 March 1939 (V42, #12).
"Card at Dealer Guest Day," *The Seed Bag*, 17 March 1937 (V37, #9).
"Community Fund Rally," *The Seed Bag*, 21 October 1938 (V41, #18).

"Everybody Welcome to Hear the Christmas Radio Program Repeated," *The Seed Bag*, 3 March 1939 (V42, #9).

"Of Interest to All Northrup-King Folks," *The Seed Bag*, 24 August 1939 (V43, #10).

"A Radio Poster," *The Seed Bag*, 3 May 1938 (V39, #14).

"Xmas Carols on December 24 Broadcast," *The Seed Bag*, 10 December 1937 (V38, #20).

"Xmas Carols on December 24 Broadcast," *The Seed Bag*, 22 December 1937 (V38, #21).

BOOKLETS, PAMPHLETS, ETC.

Clellan Card's Laugh Book, op. cit.

It Doesn't Make Sense, op. cit.

A Party Comes to Life AT DAWN, op. cit.

WCCO Radio – The Northwest's 50,000-Watt Giant, op. cit.

AUDIO-VISUAL MEDIA

"Axel's famous version of 'The Night Before Christmas,'" rec. cit.

"Kingscrost Lecture," rec. cit.

CORRESPONDENCE

Cavanor, memo. cit.

MISCELLANY

Card, "The Night Before Christmas," 1938 op. cit.

"A Channel Four Biography: Clellan Card" (WCCO-TV, circa February or March 1956).

"Clellan Card – The One Clown, Multivoiced Show," postcard cit.

"In 1936" typescript document (WCCO radio, circa 1938).

"Northrup, King & Co.'s Broadcasts Over WCCO" (Northrup, King & Company poster, circa 1938).

"Presenting – Clellan Card – A Salesman for Fels Naphtha," doc. cit.

"Program Information from Radio Sales – *Open House*" (WCCO radio, circa 1947).

Untitled typescript promotional document (WCCO radio, circa 1939).

CHAPTER 7: THE WORKING GIRL'S FRIEND

FOOTNOTES

10   The date for the origin of the Birdie has been deduced from the fact that the poem is not found in *Clellan Card's Laugh Book*, issued in April 1940, or in any other material published before 1940. However, the membership card for "Ye Ancient Order of Chestnut Chasers," circa November 1941, contains a long list of Birdies. Thus, it seems likely that Clellan began doing the bit between April 1940 and November 1941.

AUTHOR INTERVIEWS

Michael Card, Northrop "Bun" Dawson, Jr., Roger Erickson, Ernie Garven, Elaine Hogan, Jim Lavin, Dave Moore, Ellen Prin, Chuck Stanek.

INTERVIEWS BY OTHERS

Marion Card, int. cit.

BOOKS

Crews, op. cit.

Elizabeth Hough Sechrist, compiler, *One Thousand Poems for Children* (Philadelphia: Macrae Smith Co., 1946).

PERIODICALS

Adams, "In This Corner" column, *Minneapolis Star*, 19 October 1938 and 30 March 1940; and *Minneapolis Star-Journal* Minnesota section, 12 March 1944.

Johnny Dare, "On the Air ..." ad column, *Minneapolis Tribune* Classified section, 21 February 1943.

Levitan, art. cit.

Jim Richardson, "Farewell to Axel – Kids' Legend," *Suburban Life*, 27 April 1966.

"Clellan Card hosts Super-Mix Vocal-Aires," WCCO radio ad, *Minneapolis Star Journal*, 24 May 1944.

"Clellan Card's Good Humor Show Gab Session," WCCO radio ad, *Minneapolis Tribune*, 26 February 1944.

"*Curfew Time* debut over WCCO Tonight," *Minneapolis Star*, 25 September 1939.

"Heard on Land O' Lakes *Curfew Time*," *Minneapolis Star Journal*, 11 January 1940.

"Radio Comic Tops Men's Dinner Card," *Minneapolis Times*, 13 January 1940.

NEWSLETTERS

"40,000+ Laugh Books Sold Out," *The Seed Bag*, 24 May 1940 (V44, #21).

"16000 Laugh Books Ordered," *The Seed Bag*, 31 May 1940 (V44, #22).

"Card Makes a Hit with the Service Men," *The Seed Bag*, 19 March 1943 (V50, #11).

"Card Performs 'Sillyisms' at Salesmen's Dinner December 28," *The Seed Bag*, 29 December 1939 (V43, #28).

"Celebrate 1000th Radio Broadcast," *Feed Bag*, January 1940.

"Clellan Card Conducted the 1000th Program ..." *The Seed Bag*, 1 December 1939 (V43, #24).

"WAVES benefit this Saturday," *The Seed Bag*, 17 March 1944 (V52, #10).

BOOKLETS, PAMPHLETS, ETC.

Cracks by Card, op. cit.

Saturday Morning Open House Recipes.

AUDIO-VISUAL MEDIA

Dunking at the Card Table, 30 January 1946.

Super-Mix Vocal-Aires glass acetate recordings (WCCO radio broadcasts, circa 1944).

CORRESPONDENCE

Clellan Card, letter to William and Ina Card, 21 September 1923.

Michael Card, letter to the author, 29 November 1995.

Northrop "Bun" Dawson, Jr., letter to the author, 28 March 1993.

Al Sheehan, memo to Carl Burkland, 6 January 1940.

"Design for Listening! Saturday Morning Open House," sales memo.

MISCELLANY

"Presenting – Clellan Card – A Salesman for Fels Naphtha," doc. cit.

CHAPTER 8: DUNKING AT THE CARD TABLE

FOOTNOTES

11 "KSTP Option Goes Begging as Adams Inks with WCCO," *Billboard*, 29 June 1946, p. 7 (this article notes that Adams has a Hooperating of 18.9); "WCCO Drops Mpls. No. 2 Newscaster for 'Trib' Newsman," *Billboard*, 19 October 1946, p. 9 (this article states that John Raleigh, the second-highest-rated newsman, had a Hooperating of 5.1). The fact that, just a few months after the cancellation of Clellan's news show, the second-rated newscaster had a rating which was less than one-third of Adams' gives some indication of how badly Clellan was beaten in the ratings contest; radio listings for *Dunking at the Card Table* cease at about the same time.

AUTHOR INTERVIEWS

Michael Card, Ernie Garven, Jo Jones, Art Steffes, Jimmy Valentine.

INTERVIEWS BY OTHERS

Marion Card, int. cit.

BOOKS

Ingersoll, op. cit.
Millett, op. cit.

PERIODICALS

Adams, "In This Corner" column, *Minneapolis Star-Journal*, 12 March 1944.

Frank Chase, "Clellan Card To Be MC at Homecoming," *The Aquin* (College of St. Thomas paper), 28 September 1945.

Levitan, art. cit.

Richardson, art. cit.

"Cleland [*sic*] Card to Free-Lance," *Billboard*, 4 November 1944.

"Clellan Card Joins Staff at WCCO," *Minneapolis Tribune*, 1 August 1947.

"KSTP Bags Adams as Exodus from WCCO Continues," *Billboard*, 18 May 1946.

"KSTP Option Goes Begging," *Billboard*, 29 June 1946.

"Stanley Hubbard: One of the Last Originals," *Broadcasting*, 23 November 1981.

"Twin Cities, Detroit Air Studies: KSTP, WTCN, Indie Profile," *Billboard*, 4 August 1945.

"Twin Cities Outlets Ready to Cover Fair," *Billboard*, 30 August 1947.

"WCCO Continuity Director Quits to Join General Mills," *Billboard*, 8 September 1945.

NEWSLETTERS

"Doughnut Dunking Party a Great Success," *The Seed Bag*, 24 March 1944 (V52, #13).

"Early Morning Program Brings Ten Recruits for the WAVES," *Seed Trade News*, 19 April 1944.

"Extra! New Radio Program," *The Seed Bag*, 7 April 1944 (V52, #15).

BOOKLETS, PAMPHLETS, ETC.

Cracks by Card, op. cit.
Family Album (KSTP radio, circa 1942).

AUDIO-VISUAL MEDIA

Dunking at the Card Table, rec. cit.

MISCELLANY
FCC application, answer to question 34 (a listing of station personnel's salaries and duties), 1945.

Various unsourced newspaper clippings about KSTP radio, 1928.

WCCO radio studios admission tickets, 18 March & 29 April 1944.

CHAPTER 9: FROM *SPINNER SANCTUM* TO THE BOOB TUBE

FOOTNOTES
12   The same joke appears on both the *Kingscrost Lecture* transcription disk (December 1941) and a *Dunking at the Card Table* transcription disk (1 November 1945), even using the same name: Mrs. Murphy.

AUTHOR INTERVIEWS
Michael Card, Elaine Hogan, Mel Jass, Rodger Kent, Perry Martin, Dave Moore, Mary Davies Orfield, John Sieberz, Jerry Walsh, Dennis Wilfahrt.

INTERVIEWS BY OTHERS
Marion Card, int. cit.

BOOKS
Barnouw, *The Golden Web.*

DeHaven, op. cit.

Ingersoll, op. cit.

MacDonald, op. cit.

Meyer, op. cit.

Sarjeant, ed., op. cit.

PERIODICALS
Beck, art. cit.

Kid Hogan, "Channel One" column, *TV Times,* 22–28 July 1950 (Vol. 1, #9), 10–16 February 1951 (Vol. 1, #38), and 16–22 June 1951 (Vol. 2, #4).

Howard Ryan, "Axel – He's a Card," *St. Paul Pioneer Press,* 21 April 1957, *TV Tab* magazine.

Virginia Safford, "Virginia Safford" column (W.H. Card honored), *Minneapolis Star,* 25 October 1949.

Sylvia Williams, "Scratch Pad Observations" column, *TV Times,* 20–26 January 1951 (Vol. 1, #35) and 3–9 February 1951 (Vol. 1, #37).

"Card Party," WTCN radio ads, *Minneapolis Star,* June–August 1950.

"Clellan Card Midnite Show," WCCO radio ad, *Minneapolis Tribune,* 1 September 1947.

Clellan Card Show listing, *TV Times,* 26 May 1951 (Vol. 2, #1).

"Clelland [*sic*] and Dad Card Will Be School Guests," art. cit.

"Dr. Card, Pioneer Dentist, Dies," art. cit.

"Dr. W.H. Card, 71, Dies at Tonka Home," *St. Paul Dispatch,* 1 June 1950.

"Friend Card," *TV Times,* 22–28 July 1950 (Vol. 1, #9).

"Gags, Interviews, and Tin Cans on the Clellan Card Show," *TV Times,* 6–12 January 1951 (Vol. 1, #33).

"Perry Martin, 88; Professional Musician and Radio-Television Personality," *Minneapolis Star Tribune*, 12 July 1996.

"Quiz of the Twin Cities & Man on the Street" WCCO radio ad, *Minneapolis Star*, 14 October 1947.

"Quiz of the Twin Cities" WCCO radio ad, *Minneapolis Star*, 21 October 1947.

"Quiz of the Twin Cities" (Stewart MacPherson is the new host), WCCO radio ad, *Minneapolis Star*, 24 January 1950.

"Rites Set Saturday for Dr. W.H. Card," *Minneapolis Tribune*, 2 June 1950.

"Singer Honored" (W.H. Card), *Minneapolis Star*, 27 October 1949.

"Top O' the Town," WCCO radio ads, *Minneapolis Star*, June–September 1950.

"Twin Cities Outlets Ready to Cover Fair," art. cit.

"Twin Cities Show Fast TV Set Rise, Tho Not on Coax," *Billboard*, 17 June 1950.

"A Voice You Know – Clellan Card," WTCN radio ad, *Minneapolis Star*, 14 February 1951.

"WCCO Stars at the State Fair" (including Clellan), WCCO radio ad, *Minneapolis Star*, 26 August 1950.

BOOKLETS, PAMPHLETS, ETC.
Cracks by Card, op. cit.

AUDIO-VISUAL MEDIA
Card family home movies.
Flame Room Coffee Time, rec. cit.
Polka Party transcription disks, March 1955.
Various WCCO radio photos.

CORRESPONDENCE
Noel Allard, letter to the author, 2 June 1995.
William Card, letter to Mary Card, 1949.
"Program Information from Radio Sales – Clellan Card's Spinner's [sic] Sanctum" promotional memo (WCCO radio, circa 1947).

MISCELLANY
D K [Donna Kewley], "History of WCCO-TV," an unpublished chronology, August 1983.
M.A.C. Gopher, art. cit.

CHAPTER 10: THE END OF THE GOOD OLD DAYS

AUTHOR INTERVIEWS
Michael Card, William Card, Elaine Hogan, Jim Lavin, Merrill Madsen, Chuck Stanek, Stanley Tull, Jerry Walsh, Tom Welch.

PERIODICALS
Levitan, art. cit.
"2d Clellan Card Son Dies in Crash," *St. Paul Dispatch*, 6 January 1953.
"Car Death Brings Bar Crackdown," *Minneapolis Tribune*, 7 January 1953.
"Clellan Card Son Killed in Air Crash," *Minneapolis Star*, 10 September 1952.
"Clellan Card's Son, 23, Killed in Plane Crash," *Minneapolis Tribune*, 10 September 1952.
"Clellan Card's Son Killed in Car Accident," *Minneapolis Star*, 6 January 1953.

Clellan Peter Card obituary, *Minneapolis Tribune*, 12 September 1952.

"Crash Kills Son of Clellan Card," *St. Paul Pioneer Press*, 10 September 1952.

"Gags, Interviews, and Tin Cans on the Clellan Card Show," art. cit.

John B. Card obituary, *Minneapolis Tribune*, 8 January 1953.

"Rites Friday for John Card," *Minneapolis Star*, 7 January 1953.

CORRESPONDENCE

Allard, letter cit.

Michael Card, letter cit.

MISCELLANY

The Kaydet (St. Thomas yearbook), 1946 and 1952.

Report of Special Investigation of Major Aircraft Accident on 9 September 1952 (U.S. War Department, 26 September 1952).

Clellan P. Card transcript, University of Minnesota, 1947–1950.

CHAPTER 11: BIRDIE, THY NAME IS TORGESON

FOOTNOTES

13   The name was sometimes spelled "Torgenson" or "Torgerson," but "Torgeson" is the most common spelling.

14   Compare Tena singing "Way Down Upon the Swanson River" in the transcribed excerpt of an episode of *Tena and Tim* featured in *The 30th Anniversary of WCCO Radio* (broadcast 21 October 1954) with Axel singing the same song on *Axel and His Dog* (10 July 1955).

AUTHOR INTERVIEWS

Michael Card, Mel Jass, Jim Lavin, Dave Moore, David Prin, John Prin, Chuck Stanek, Don Stolz.

INTERVIEWS BY OTHERS

Don Stolz, conducted by Terry Fisk and Laura Boyce, October 1983.

Don Stolz, conducted by Mark J. Hinsted, autumn 1992.

Don Stolz, conducted by Kristian Berg, October 1994.

BOOKS

DeHaven, op. cit.

Dunning, op. cit.

Sarjeant, ed., op. cit.

Williams and Hartley, op. cit.

PERIODICALS

Beck, art. cit.

Dick Chapman, "Nostalgia," *Mpls.*, August 1975.

"Channel One" column, *TV Guide and Forecast*, 21 March 1953 (Vol. 3, #44).

"Ticket Drive Starts," *Minneapolis Tribune*, 14 September 1955.

NEWSLETTERS

Telepulse, April–June 1952.

BOOKLETS, PAMPHLETS, ETC.
WCCO radio rate booklet, May 1953.
Inside WCCO Television, 1949–1974 (WCCO-TV, 1974).

AUDIO-VISUAL MEDIA
Clellan Card, Gold Medal Flour messages on transcription disk (WCCO radio, circa 1953).
The 30th Anniversary of WCCO Radio, rec. cit.
Axel, prog. cit. (December 1964–January 1965).
Axel's "The Night Before Christmas," rec. cit.
The Mel Jass Show television program audio recordings (WCCO-TV, date unknown (1 April 1955?)).
Polka Party transcription disks (WCCO radio, April 1953, March 1955, etc.).
Pop the Question transcription disks (WCCO radio, April 1953).
Roundy Predicts kinescope (WCCO-TV, undated (circa 1964?)).
WCCO-TV photos, circa 1955–1956.

MISCELLANY
D K [Donna Kewley], op. cit.
Radio schedules, 1953–1954.

CHAPTER 12: THE BIRTH OF *AXEL AND HIS DOG*

FOOTNOTES
15   The *Variety* review of the first episode does not mention an off-color joke so it may be that this incident did not happen on that particular show. However, on *Axel and His Dog* on Saturday, September 3, 1955, when Tallulah asked, "Do you know why the chicken crossed the road?" Axel mentioned knowing "several wersions" of it and seemed to be sharing a private joke with Tallulah, which suggests that this event really did happen, but perhaps on some other early episode of the program rather than on the very first broadcast.

AUTHOR INTERVIEWS
Bill Dietrichson, Harry Jones, Don Stolz, Jimmy Valentine.

INTERVIEWS BY OTHERS
Harry Jones, conducted by Terry Fisk and Laura Boyce, September 1983.
Mary Davies Orfield, conducted by Terry Fisk and Laura Boyce, October 1983.
Don Stolz, int. cit. (1983).

BOOKS
Aden, op. cit.
Davis, op. cit.
Fischer, op. cit.
Grossman, op. cit.
Hollis, *Hi There, Boys and Girls!*
Ingram, op. cit.

PERIODICALS
Chase, art. cit.

Angelo Cohn, "Old Log's 'Stepfather' Recalls Theater's Lean Days," *Minneapolis Star*, 30 November 1960.

Carol Honsa, "Old Log Theater Here to Stay," *Minneapolis Star*, 16 June 1964.

Jones, "After Last Night" column, *Minneapolis Tribune*, 3 August 1954.

Clifford Nyeberg, "Old Log Theater," *Minneapaulitan Magazine*, July 1960.

Merle Potter, "Your Times as Seen by Merle Potter," *Minneapolis Daily Times*, 12 June 1941.

Tom Ratzloff, "Performer Who Played Axel's 'Tallulah' Recalls Popular TV Show," *The Old Times*, February 1994.

Ryan, art. cit.

Dan Sullivan, "Old Log: A Success Story," *Minneapolis Tribune*, 21 June 1964.

"Axel and His Dog," *Variety*, art. cit.

"Casey Jones Scores with Mama," *TV Guide*, 31 July 1954.

"Channel One," *TV Forecast*, 14 February 1953 (Vol. 3, #39).

"Harry Jones," *TV Times*, 30 September–6 October 1950 (Vol. 1, #19).

"Hi-Notes in Fashion," *TV Guide* (Northwest ed.), 22 May 1953 (Vol. 1, #8).

"Jimmy's Junior Jamboree," *Twin Cities Tele-Viewer*, 30 April–13 May 1950 (Vol. 1, #1).

"Jimmy's Junior Jamboree," *TV Times*, 6–12 January 1951 (Vol. 1, #33).

"Toby Prin," *Twin Cities Tele-Viewer*, 14–31 May 1950 (Vol. 1, #2).

"Town Toppers" column, *Minneapolis Star*, 9 June 1952.

"Town Toppers" column, *Minneapolis Star*, 6 February 1958.

NEWSLETTERS
Pavek Museum of Broadcasting Newsletter, May–July 1996.

BOOKLETS, PAMPHLETS, ETC.
Inside WCCO Television, op. cit

A Score for 4: 1949–1969, op. cit.

AUDIO-VISUAL MEDIA
Axel and His Dog, prog. cit., 1955–1956.

Card, "Kings X Lecture," rec. cit.

Casey's Comedy Album for Kids, rec. cit.

Kids' TV Nostalgia Hour, prog. cit.

Roundy Predicts, prog. cit.

WCCO-TV photos, August 1954–March 1955.

MISCELLANY
"Axel Day," scrapbook cit.

Terry Fisk, unpublished data.

Pufall, op. cit.

Show Offs file at the Minnesota History Center (WTCN-TV, circa May 1951).

CHAPTER 13: AXEL AND HIS NURSE (AND SOME MORE AMINALS)

FOOTNOTES

16 During most of the run of *Axel and His Dog*, this drawing of the tree, including the sign inscribed "Axel's Tree House," served as the opening shot. This has given rise to the mistaken idea that the name of the show was *Axel's Tree House* or even *Axel and His Tree House* (e.g. Bob DeHaven, *55 Years Before the Mike* (Minneapolis: James D. Thueson, 1985) p. 41; *Axel and His Tree House*, Tape 1 (1955) and Tape 2 (1956) (Minneapolis: Pavek Museum of Broadcasting videotapes, 1992); Kristine M. Holmgren, "He moved slowly so we'd catch up," *Minneapolis Tribune*, Sunday 28 March 1993, p. 25A). Even Don Stolz, the "dog" of *Axel and His Dog*, has sometimes referred to the show as *Axel's Tree House*. Although in the last years of the show, the name often reflected the current film package (*Axel and Bomba, Axel and Deputy Dawg*) or was simply abbreviated to *Axel*, for nearly a decade the official title was *Axel and His Dog*. The program was never called *Axel's Tree House* in *TV Guide* or the television logs of the local newspapers.

17 The date of Tallulah's debut has been deduced from the available evidence. Don Stolz and Harry Jones agree that Tallulah was not part of *Axel and His Dog* when it began; the *Variety* review of the premiere and the August 1954 ad tend to corroborate this, since neither makes any mention of Tallulah. However, the cat was featured on the show by October 8, because her white paw is visible in photographs that are known to have been taken on that date. Therefore, Tallulah must have been created sometime between August 5 and October 8, 1954. Since the show initially ran only once a week, and presumably a few episodes had aired before the need for another character became acute, a September date for Tallulah's first appearance seems most probable.

18 Harry Jones didn't remember receiving any dirty jokes in the mail, but Don Stolz and Michael Card both recalled that an occasional one came in. Neither believed that it was done maliciously, but rather that the kids simply didn't understand the off-color humor and only knew that the jokes were supposed to be funny.

19 The date when Clellan was stricken must have been after October 12, because at that time he was still scheduled to be on WCCO radio's thirtieth anniversary show (Jones, "After Last Night" column, *Minneapolis Tribune*, 13 October 1954, p. 29). On the other hand, it must have been before October 22, because notices of his illness (and Mary Davies' new role) appeared in the columns of both Adams and Jones on that date (Adams,"In This Corner" column, *Minneapolis Star*, 22 October 1954, p. 50; Jones, "After Last Night" column, *Minneapolis Tribune*, 22 October 1954, p. 33). Adams also noted that it happened "recently," indicating a date not long before October 22. A list of Clellan's service dates as a patient at Abbott Hospital shows that the only discharge date which could possibly fit is October 16, 1954. The actual records are lost, but the logical inference is that Clellan fell ill between the 13th and 16th. Considering his ailment, it's likely that he had a short hospital stay, so Friday, October 15, seems a reasonable guess for the date of Carmen's debut.

AUTHOR INTERVIEWS

Michael Card, Bill Dietrichson, Harry Jones, Mary Davies Orfield, Don Stolz.

INTERVIEWS BY OTHERS

Harry Jones, int. cit. (1983).

Mary Davies Orfield, int. cit. (1983).

Mary Davies Orfield, conducted by Mark J. Hinsted, autumn 1992.

Mary Davies Orfield, conducted by Kristian Berg, October 1994.

Bob Pratt, conducted by Kristian Berg, November 1994.

NOTES

PERIODICALS

Adams, "In This Corner" column, *Minneapolis Star*, 22 October 1954.

T.L. Ayers, "Labs Work on Different TV," *St. Paul Pioneer Press*, 26 December 1954.

Janet Grant, "Color Her Ch. 4's Mary Davies," *TV Times*, 12 November 1966 (Vol. 7, #27) and 26 November 1966 (Vol. 7, #29).

Jones, "After Last Night" column, *Minneapolis Tribune*, 8 October, 13 October, 22 October, and 24 December 1954.

Ryan, art. cit.

"1st Color TV from Twin Cities," *Hastings* (MN) *Gazette*, 24 December 1954.

"Axel and His Dog," *Variety*, art. cit.

"Color Comes to the Twin Cities," *Technician-Engineer*, February 1955.

"Sparkling Lively New Comedy!" WCCO-TV ad, *TV Guide*, 14–20 August 1954.

"TV in Minneapolis: Salesmen to 500,000 Families," *Greater Minneapolis*, November 1954.

NEWSLETTERS

[Julie Moden and Carol Schaubach], "Merry Christmas!" *Tree House Tribune*, December 1966 (unnumbered).

[Schaubach], "Carmen: Mary Davies," *Tree House Tribune*, May 1965 (Vol. 1, #4).

"Axel to Have New Pet in His Tree House," *Views from Channel 4*, January 1955 (Vol. 2, #1).

Telepulse, August 1954–April 1955.

BOOKLETS, PAMPHLETS, ETC.

Inside WCCO Television, op. cit

A Score for 4: 1949–1969, op. cit.

AUDIO-VISUAL MEDIA

The 30th Anniversary of WCCO Radio, rec. cit.

Arthur Godfrey's Talent Scouts television program, 9 July 1955.

Axel and His Dog, prog. cit., 1955–1956.

Carmen, prog. cit., 25 March 1977.

Country Holiday, prog. cit.

WCCO-TV photos, 1954–1960.

CORRESPONDENCE

Unsigned memo (WCCO-TV, dated 5:30 p.m., 8 October 1954).

MISCELLANY

Mary Davies, "Autobiography of Mary Davies," unpublished typescript manuscript, undated (circa January 1960).

D K [Donna Kewley], op. cit.

CHAPTER 14: PEWTIN' DOWN ROOTS IN DA TREE HOUSE

FOOTNOTES

20 The date has been deduced from the two earliest surviving episodes of *Axel and His Dog*, dated March 5 and March 12, 1955, on the film leaders. In the first program, the

original tree is still in use; in the second, the familiar crotch of the tree stands in the foreground. The new tree trunk must have been installed sometime between March 5 and March 12 – most likely on Monday, March 7.

AUTHOR INTERVIEWS
Tom Cousins, Bill Dietrichson, Harry Jones, Mary Davies Orfield, Don Pottratz, Don Stolz, Stan Wolfson.

INTERVIEWS BY OTHERS
Harry Jones, int. cit. (1983).
Bob Pratt, int. cit.
Don Stolz, int. cit. (1983).
Don Stolz, int. cit. (1992).

BOOKS
Maltin and Bann, op. cit.

PERIODICALS
Jones, "After Last Night" column, *Minneapolis Tribune*, 28 April and 17 May 1955.
"Baby Daughter of Don Stolz Dies in Tonka," *Minneapolis Tribune*, 4 August 1955.
"Cooler Air Moving into Region," *Minneapolis Star*, 4 August 1955.
"Daughter of Theater Man Drowns," *Minneapolis Star*, 4 August 1955.
"Town Toppers" column, *Minneapolis Star*, 6 February 1958.

NEWSLETTERS
Telepulse, October 1954–April 1955.

BOOKLETS, PAMPHLETS, ETC.
Tom Stolz, *Axel and His Dog* play program (Great American History Theatre, 1998).
WCCO Radio – The Northwest's 50,000-Watt Giant, op. cit.

AUDIO-VISUAL MEDIA
The 30th Anniversary of WCCO Radio, rec. cit.
Axel and His Dog, prog. cit., 1955–1957, 1965.
First Bank Notes audition tape recordings (WCCO radio, 1955–1956).
WCCO-TV photos, August 1954–December 1955.

MISCELLANY
Pufall, op. cit.

CHAPTER 15: FRIED ICE AND DOUGHNUT HOLES

FOOTNOTES
21 Sources: *Carmen*, WCCO-TV, videotape recording, 1 July 1974; Don Stolz, October 1983; Don Stolz, autumn 1992; Don Stolz, January 1993; Don Stolz, October 1994; Don Stolz, January 1997. As can be seen from the list above, Don has told this story a number of times. Most recently, he has said that the theater's clock was off by an hour due to a change to daylight savings time, and that this made Clellan an hour late. In an earlier version of the tale (from 1983), Don claimed simply that the clock had stopped. However, the earliest available account of the incident is from the 1 July 1974 episode of *Carmen*. On that program, Don declared, "I remember one time [Clellan] went to a motion

picture and slept through the show. Really. Tallulah and Towser did the whole thing ....
He showed up when it was over and he thought he was just in time for rehearsal." Since
that statement was made relatively soon after the actual event, it's likely that is what
really happened. Don more or less confirmed this in an interview with the author in January 1997.

AUTHOR INTERVIEWS
Harry Jones, Mary Davies Orfield, Don Pottratz, Don Stolz.

INTERVIEWS BY OTHERS
Don Stolz, int. cit. (1983).
Don Stolz, int. cit. (1992).
Don Stolz, int. cit. (1994).

PERIODICALS
"Unburied Treasure for Every Sponsor," WCCO-TV ad, *Sponsor Fall Facts*, 1957.
Television Magazine, August 1957.
TV & Radio Basics, July 1957.

NEWSLETTERS
[Mary Davies], "Carmen's Column," *Tree House Tribune*, January 1966 (Vol. I, #11).

AUDIO-VISUAL MEDIA
Axel and His Dog, prog. cit., 1955–1957, December 1964–March 1965.
Axel "Goodie Reel," prog. cit.
Carmen, prog. cit. (1974).
WCCO-TV photos, 1956–1960.

MISCELLANY
John Gallos personal appearance at a meeting of the Block-Heads tent of The Sons of the
Desert (Laurel and Hardy Fan Club), 8 December 1996.

CHAPTER 17: MAGIC ISLAND MISDEMEANORS

AUTHOR INTERVIEWS
William Card, Tom Cousins, Bill Dietrichson, Mary Davies Orfield, Don Stolz, Stan Wolfson.

INTERVIEWS BY OTHERS
Bob Pratt, int. cit.
Don Stolz, int. cit. (1983).
Don Stolz, int. cit. (1992).

BOOKS
Meyer, op. cit.

PERIODICALS
Jones, "After Last Night" column, *Minneapolis Tribune*, 20 December 1957.
"Amusement Park Gives Away Cigars on Fathers' Day," *Minnetonka Record*, 16 June
1960.

"Axel, Clancy to Be at Excelsior Park on Sunday," *Minnetonka Record*, 20 September 1962.

"Axel's Birthday at Park Sunday," *Minnetonka Record*, 7 September 1961.

"Fireworks Display at Excelsior Park Sunday Night," *Minnetonka Record*, 26 May 1960.

"Rides for Good Marks," *Minnetonka Record*, 4 June 1964.

"WCCO Personalities at Excelsior Park for 'Report Card' Days," *Minnetonka Record*, 6 June 1963.

NEWSLETTERS

"No Lost Kids Left Over," *Views from Channel 4*, July 1959 (Vol. 6, #5).

BOOKLETS, PAMPHLETS, ETC.

"Axel and Deputy Dawg with Live Studio Audience" promotional flyer (WCCO-TV, July 1963).

AUDIO-VISUAL MEDIA

Axel and His Dog, prog. cit., 1955–1957, December 1964.

Axel "Goodie Reel," prog. cit.

Clellan Card's Humor, prog. cit.

WCCO-TV photos, 1958–1961, 1965.

MISCELLANY

ARBitron ratings data, January 1959–December 1961.

Axel postcard (Hiawatha Color Advertising Company, 1964).

CHAPTER 18: CARMEN GET IT!

FOOTNOTES

22   Morris, "A New Old Log Theater is Taking Shape," *Minneapolis Star*, 18 August 1960, p. 1C; Bob Murphy, "'Old Log' Neither Old Nor Log," *Minneapolis Star*, 16 November 1960, p. 1B; Cohn, "Old Log's 'Stepfather'," *Minneapolis Star*, 30 November 1960, p. 1B. These sources give the cost as $150,000, though others list the outlay as $250,000 (e.g., "Work Starts Immediately on 'New Log'," *Minneapolis Star*, 17 February 1960, p. 1B; Honsa, "Old Log Theater Here to Stay," *Minneapolis Star*, 16 June 1964, p. 1B; Sullivan, "Old Log: A Success Story," *Minneapolis Tribune*, 21 June 1964, p. E5). Don Stolz explained the discrepancy by noting that the smaller figure included only the cost of erecting the building itself; technical equipment, furnishings, and other expenses accounted for the remainder of the $250,000 total (Don Stolz, interview with the author, 19 March 1997).

23   Unfortunately, because no official announcement was ever made, there is no documentation proving precisely when Don left *Axel and His Dog*. The date of Don's departure from the show has been deduced from the available evidence. Photographs verify that he was still on the program in September 1961. In late March 1962, the show was retitled *Axel and Rocky* to capitalize on their newly-acquired film product ("Axel Meets Rocky," WCCO-TV ad, *Minneapolis Tribune*, 26 March 1962). This also may be an indication that the dog (i.e., Don) of *Axel and His Dog* had left – after all, the show had never been retitled *Axel and the Little Rascals*, despite the huge audience appeal of the Roach kids. The kinescope of *Axel and His Dog* from June 4, 1962, depicts Axel calling to Tallulah, but there is no audible response, also suggesting that Don was not there. In September 1962, it was announced that *Bomba the Jungle Boy* would replace *Axel and His Dog* (Forrest Powers, "TV-Radio Chatter" column, *Minneapolis Star*, 7 September 1962, p. 17B); it may be that Don's absence even prompted thoughts of cancelling *Axel and His Dog*.

In the event, Axel remained and the show was retitled *Axel and Bomba* – and then a few months later, featuring a new film package, *Axel and the Bowery Boys*. All these clues suggest that Don left the show around the spring of 1962. Indeed, the *Minneapolis Tribune*, the *Minneapolis Star*, and *TV Guide* all list the weekday show as *Axel and His Dog* for the final time on March 23, 1962, which tends to support a spring 1962 departure date for Don but is not conclusive. On the other hand, all three publications continue to list the Saturday (or, toward the end, Sunday) version of the show as *Axel and His Dog*, until the weekend listing ceases after Sunday, October 20, 1963. This might indicate that Don continued to do the weekend show for a year or so after he stopped doing the weekday version.

24 Again, because documentation is extremely sparse, the date is an educated guess. Don was definitely gone by March 1963, according to director Ken Pack who joined WCCO-TV that month (interview, 6 August 1997; this is confirmed by Mel Tollefson who joined WCCO-TV in July 1963 (interview, 19 October 1995)). Don certainly left well before Easter 1963, because Carmen seems to have become Axel's partner by then (1963 Dayton's Bunny Breakfast photo trading card), and that didn't happen until after Don had been absent for a while (Harry Jones interview, 30 July 1995). By the fall of 1963, advertisements clearly portray Axel and Carmen as co-hosts (*e.g.* "Axel and His Nurse Carmen Have Great Fun with Deputy Dawg," *TV Times*, 12 October 1963 (Vol. 4, #22), p. 32).

25 In fact, when Mary relates this story, she often can't remember the correct punchline. The July 1, 1974 episode of *Carmen* has the most coherent version.

AUTHOR INTERVIEWS
Harry Jones, Allan Lotsberg, Mary Davies Orfield, Ken Pack, Don Stolz, Mel Tollefson, Stan Wolfson.

INTERVIEWS BY OTHERS
Allan Lotsberg, conducted by Mark J. Hinsted, autumn 1992.
Mary Davies Orfield, conducted by Charlie Anderson, 1992.

BOOKS
Fischer, op. cit.
Leonard Maltin, *Movie and Video Guide 1995* (New York: Signet, 1995).

PERIODICALS
Card, "One Man's Opinion," *Minnetonka Record*, 28 June, 2 August, and 23 August 1962.
Cohn, art. cit.
George Grim, "I Like It Here" column, *Minneapolis Tribune*, 13 February 1961.
Honsa, art. cit.
Roger LaFayette, "Inside TeeVeeLand" column, *TV Times*, 7–13 September 1963 (Vol. 4, #17).
LaFayette, "Inside TeeVeeLand" column ("Will WCCO Christmas record be a hit or miss?"), *TV Times*, 12–18 December 1964 (Vol. 5, #31).
Morris, art. cit.
Murphy, art. cit.
Powers, art. cit.
John K. Sherman, "Words and Music" column ("New Old Log Is off to a Splendid Start"), *Minneapolis Star*, 1 December 1960.
Sullivan, art. cit.
ARBitron ratings data, *Variety*, 13 February, 3 April, and 15 May 1963.

"Axel and His Nurse Carmen Have Great Fun with Deputy Dawg," art. cit.

"Axel Meets Rocky," WCCO-TV ad, *Minneapolis Tribune*, 26 March 1962.

"Axel Starts 10th Year as Favorite of Children," *Minnetonka Record*, 14 November 1963.

"Clellan Card Starts Column for Record," *Minnetonka Record*, 7 June 1962.

"An Exciting New Season for KIDS Starring BOMBA the Jungle Boy" WCCO-TV ad, *TV Guide* (Twin Cities edition), 15–21 September 1962.

"For Fun and Adventure, it's Axel and the Bowery Boys" WCCO-TV ad, *TV Times*, 17–23 August 1963 (Vol. 4, #14).

"From the Production Centres," *Variety*, 19 September 1962.

"Hey! Kids! Get Your Very Own AXEL Today!" WCCO-TV ad, *Minnetonka Record*, 14 November 1963.

"Nothing but Trees!," *Greater Minneapolis*, April 1963.

St. Paul ACE Magazine, April 1963.

"Town Toppers" column, *Minneapolis Star*, 9 June 1952.

"Work Starts Immediately on 'New Log'," art. cit.

AUDIO-VISUAL MEDIA

Axel, prog. cit., June 1962, December 1964–March 1965.

"Axel's Famous Version of 'The Night Before Christmas'" b/w "Close Call for Santa" phonograph record.

Carmen, prog. cit., 1 July 1974.

Clancy and Willie, prog. cit., 25 March 1977.

Julie Moden Enroth photo collection, circa 1965–1967.

"The Lonesome Road" and *Zounds! What Sounds!* liner notes, as reproduced in *Incredibly Strange Music, Volume I* compact disc (Caroline Records, 1993).

WCCO-TV photos, 1962.

MISCELLANY

D K [Donna Kewley], op. cit.

Pufall, op. cit.

Thomes, doc. cit.

Axel photo trading card, circa 1964.

Dayton's Bunny Breakfast photo trading card (Dayton's/WCCO-TV, 1963).

"Note from the Tree House" included with Axel doll, (WCCO-TV, 1963).

CHAPTER 19: PRESIDENT AXEL

AUTHOR INTERVIEWS

Julie Moden Enroth, Wally Green, Mary Davies Orfield, Carol Schaubach.

BOOKS

Grossman, op. cit.

NEWSLETTERS

[Moden], "Axel: Clellan Card," *Tree House Tribune*, May 1965 (Vol. 1, #4).

"Axel Runs for President, Carmen for Vice-Pres.," *Tree House Tribune*, June 1965 (Vol. 1, #5).

"Bobo Reports," *Tree House Tribune*, July-August 1965 (Vol. 1, #6).

"Grandma Torgeson's Column," *Tree House Tribune*, June 1965 (Vol. 1, #5).
"Hi There!" *Tree House Tribune*, March 1966 (Vol. 1, #13).
"Life with Axel," *Tree House Tribune*, June 1965 (Vol. 1, #5).
Tree House Tribune, February 1965 (Vol. 1, #1).

AUDIO-VISUAL MEDIA
Axel, prog. cit., December 1964–March 1965.
WCCO-TV photos, 1965.

MISCELLANY
Moden, op. cit.
ARBitron ratings data, 1956, 1959, and 1964.
"The Axel and Carmen Fan Club" scrapbook, op. cit.
Axel postcard, 1964.
WCCO-TV sales info, 23 December 1964.

CHAPTER 20: "TELL 'EM I'M GOING AROUND THE WORLD"

FOOTNOTES
26 A photo in the book *Holy Cow! The Life and Times of Halsey Hall* by Stew Thornley (Minneapolis: Nodin Press, 1991), shows Clellan, Roundy Coughlin, Halsey Hall, and Dick Cullum on the set. The caption implies that the photo was taken in 1964. However, the negative (WCCO-TV #8-76) is dated 15 September 1965, which was the show's season premiere. There is no evidence that Clellan was featured on *Roundy Predicts* prior to 1965; for example, he is not mentioned in the program's advertising in 1964 (*e.g. Roundy Predicts* WCCO-TV ad, *TV Times*, 17–23 October 1964 (Vol. 5, #23), p. 28).
27 At least according to Dick Chapman in "Nostalgia," *Mpls.*, August 1975, p. 70. Chapman incorrectly states that Clellan's death was in 1963 and his one-page article is riddled with other errors – notably the claim that Axel's dog was named "Bowzer"(!!) – but this anecdote has the ring of truth.

AUTHOR INTERVIEWS
Dennis Blenis, Michael Card, William Card, Maurice Crowley, Corey Gordon, Allan Lotsberg, Dr. James L. McKenna, Maryann McKenna, Mary Davies Orfield, David Prin, Dr. A. Boyd Thomes.

INTERVIEWS BY OTHERS
Allan Lotsberg, int. cit.
Mary Davies Orfield, int. cit. (1983).
Mary Davies Orfield, int. cit. (1992).
Bob Pratt, int. cit.

PERIODICALS
Card, "One Man's Opinion," *Minnetonka Record*, 12 July 1962.
Card (quoting Zane Grey), "One Man's Opinion" column, *Minnetonka Record*, 23 August 1962.
Chapman, art. cit.
Suzanne Hovik, "'Biggest Backyard Carnival' has Its 6th Successful Year," *Minneapolis Star*, 15 August 1969.
"Cancer Carnival," *Minneapolis Star*, 15 August 1967.

"Clellan Card," *St. Paul Pioneer Press*, 14 April 1966.

"Clellan Card Buried April 16 from St. John's," *Minnetonka Herald*, 21 April 1966.

"Clellan Card, TV's Axel, Dies of Cancer at 62," *St. Paul Dispatch*, 13 April 1966.

"Premiere Tonight: 'Roundy Predicts' Football Prognosticator Roundy Coughlin Features Fun with Halsey Hall and Clellan Card" WCCO-TV ad, *TV Times*, 11–17 September 1965 (Vol. 6, #18).

"Radio, TV Performer Clellan Card Dies," *Minneapolis Tribune*, Thursday 14 April 1966.

"'Roundy Predicts' Football Fun with Roundy Coughlin, Halsey Hall, and Clellan Card" WCCO-TV ad, *TV Times*, 18–24 September 1965 (Vol. 6, #19).

NEWSLETTERS

[Clellan Card], "Axel's Column," *Tree House Tribune*, February 1966 (Vol. 1, #12).

[Mary Davies], "A Note from Carmen," *Tree House Tribune*, June 1966 (Vol. 11, #2).

AUDIO-VISUAL MEDIA

WCCO-TV photos, 1961–1965.

WEB SITES

www.mnkidvid.com/twincities/wcco/axel/memory.html.

MISCELLANY

Clellan C. Card Certificate of Death (Minnesota Department of Health, 14 April 1966).

Michael Card, family genealogy.

C. W. Freeman, "Surgical Pathology Report: Clellan Card," 12 July 1965.

Moden, op. cit.

Thomes, doc. cit.

"$5,630 Given to Clellan Card Memorial Fund," American Cancer Society press release, 15 July 1966.

"The Axel and Carmen Fan Club" scrapbook, op. cit.

"Bill Carlson – Gwen Harvey – Clellan Card" photo trading card (WCCO-TV), circa 1965.

Nurse's notes, Abbot Hospital, 1 December 1965.

Physical examination, Abbott Hospital, 21 July 1944.

Record of Funeral, Huber-Lee funeral home, April 1966.

Service dates for Clelland [*sic*] C. Card, Abbott Hospital.

AFTERWORD: AFTERWARD

FOOTNOTES

28 Actually, it was twenty-two and a half years – but her claim to be the longest-term children's personality in the Twin Cities is probably true, although she was on the air as Carmen only sporadically for the first nine years or so.

AUTHOR INTERVIEWS

Corey Gordon, Pete Hautman, Harry Jones, Allan Lotsberg, Dave Moore, Mary Davies Orfield, Don Stolz.

BOOKS

Grossman, op. cit.

Pete Hautman, *The Mortal Nuts* (New York: Simon & Schuster, 1996).

PERIODICALS

Noel Holston, "Profit and Loss," *Star Tribune*, 4 May 1995.

Jones, "After Last Night" column, *Minneapolis Tribune*, 8 May 1975.

Irv Letofsky (substituting for Jones), "After Last Night" column, *Minneapolis Tribune*, 30 December 1972.

Margery Martin, "It Was a Television Premiere for Kathy Abel of Minnetonka," *Hopkins-Minnetonka-Eden Prairie Sun*, 13 October 1976.

Michael Phillips, "Doggy Treats," *St. Paul Pioneer Press*, 28 September 1998.

Graydon Royce, "This Week's Best Bets: Theater: 'Axel & His Dog'," *Minneapolis Star Tribune*, 3 October 2003.

Graydon Royce, "Real Strength of 'Axel' Turns on Fond Memories," *Minneapolis Star Tribune*, 7 October 2003.

Jarrett Smith, "A Dogged Friendship," *Minneapolis Star Tribune*, 3 October 1998.

"Bulletin Board" column, *St. Paul Pioneer Press*, 17–25 March 1993.

"The Hosts of Kids' Shows Glowed in Golden Era of Twin Cities Television," *Minneapolis Tribune Picture Magazine*, 3 June 1984.

NEWSLETTERS

Pavek Museum of Broadcasting Newsletter, June–July 2008.

AUDIO-VISUAL MEDIA

Carmen, prog. cit., 25 March 1977.

Clancy and Willie, prog. cit., 25 March 1977.

Clellan Card's Humor, prog. cit.

Lunch with Casey, prog. cit., audio recording, 29 December 1972.

Lost Twin Cities II, prog. cit.

WEB SITES

www.lunchwithcasey.com.

www.mnkidvid.com.

www.tvparty.com/lostkids.html.

www.myspace.com/stevealmaas.

CORRESPONDENCE

Michael Card, email to the author, 24 October 2007.

MISCELLANY

Marc Johnson, "Ink Heads, Part 1," 1995.

D K [Donna Kewley], op. cit.

Pufall, op. cit.

Birdie with a yellow bill
Hopped upon my windowsill,
Cocked his shining eye and said:
Hey, I hear you read a book – Mark!
Bee boop!